DOMINI REPUBLIC TRAVEL GUIDE

2024

55+ Fun Things to Do in and Around Dominican Republic

Taylor Allen

All rights reserved. No part of this book may be reproduced, stored in a retrieval system, or transmitted in any form or by any means, electronic, mechanical, photocopying, recording, or otherwise, without the prior written permission of the copyright owner. The information contained in this book is for general information purposes only. The author and publisher make no representations or warranties of any kind, express or implied, about the completeness, accuracy, reliability, suitability or availability with respect to the book or the information, products, services, or related graphics contained in the book for any purpose. Any reliance you place on such information is therefore strictly at your own risk.

Copyright © 2023 by Taylor Allen.

TABLE OF CONTENT

Chapter 1: Introduction to the Dominican Republic 7
    Overview of the Country _____ 8
    1Cultural Insights _____ 9
    Getting Around _____ 11

Chapter 2: Beach Adventures 15
    Relaxing on Punta Cana Beach _____ 15
    Exploring Bahia de las Aguilas _____ 16
    Kite Surfing in Cabarete _____ 18
    Snorkeling in Saona Island _____ 20
    Beachcombing in Bahia de las Calderas _____ 22

Chapter 3: Historical Marvels 25
    Visiting the Zona Colonial in Santo Domingo ___ 25
    Discovering the Ruins of Altos de Chavón ____ 27
    Exploring Fort San Felipe in Puerto Plata ____ 29
    El Faro Lighthouse in Punta Rucia _____ 31
    Taino Caves in Los Haitises National Park ___ 33

Chapter 4: Outdoor Adventures 37
    Hiking Pico Duarte, the Caribbean's Highest Peak __ 37
    Zip-Lining in the Anamuya Mountains _____ 38
    White-Water Rafting in Jarabacoa _____ 40
    Horseback Riding in Constanza Valley _____ 42
    Caving in Los Haitises National Park _____ 44

Chapter 5: Culinary Delights 47
    Savoring Mangu and Other Traditional Dishes __ 47
    Experiencing the Flavors of Mofongo _____ 48

  Sampling Street Food in Santiago _____ 50
  Dominican Coffee Tasting in Jarabacoa _____ 52
  Chocolate Making Workshops in Puerto Plata _____ 54

Chapter 6: Cultural Immersion _____ 57
  Attending a Merengue or Bachata Dance Workshop _ 57
  Exploring the Larimar Mines in Barahona _____ 59
  Visiting a Dominican Cigar Factory _____ 61
  Artisan Craft Markets in Santo Domingo _____ 62
  Traditional Festivals and Celebrations _____ 64

Chapter 7: Water Activities _____ 67
  Diving in Bayahibe's Coral Reefs _____ 67
  Whale Watching in Samaná _____ 68
  Catamaran Tours in Punta Cana _____ 70
  Fishing Excursions in Cabo Rojo _____ 72
  Surfing in Encuentro Beach _____ 74

Chapter 8: Relaxation and Wellness _____ 77
  Spa Retreats in Punta Cana _____ 77
  Yoga and Meditation in Las Galeras _____ 78
  Hot Springs in La Ciénaga _____ 81
  Natural Mud Baths in Barahona _____ 82
  Beachfront Massages in Juan Dolio _____ 84

Chapter 9: Nightlife and Entertainment _____ 87
  Salsa Dancing in Santo Domingo _____ 87
  Beach Parties in Punta Cana _____ 89
  Jazz and Blues in Cabarete _____ 90
  Casino Nights in Santo Domingo _____ 92
  Live Music in Puerto Plata _____ 94

Chapter 10: Wildlife Encounters ... 97
- Visiting the Jaragua National Park ... 97
- Birdwatching in Los Haitises ... 98
- Exploring the Cotubanamá National Park ... 100
- Dolphin Encounters in Punta Cana ... 102
- Turtle Watching in Bahia de las Aguilas ... 103

Chapter 11: Hidden Gems and Off-the-Beaten-Path Adventures ... 105
- Exploring the Remote Playa Rincón ... 105
- Hiking to the El Limón Waterfall ... 107
- Discovering the Magic of Bahoruco ... 109
- Laguna El Dudú: A Natural Wonder ... 111
- Remote Villages and Cultural Experiences ... 112

Chapter 12: Adventure Sports and Extreme Activities ... 115
- Paragliding Over Jarabacoa Valley ... 115
- Deep-Sea Diving in Bayahibe ... 117
- ATV Off-Roading Adventures ... 118
- Kitesurfing on the North Coast ... 120
- Canyoning in the El Limón Canyon ... 122

Chapter 13: Tips for Travelers ... 125
- Packing Essentials ... 125
- Safety and Health Considerations ... 127
- Language and Communication Tips ... 129
- Transportation Tips ... 131
- Recommended Reading and Resources ... 133

Chapter 14: Travel Itinerary ... 137

Family Friendly Itinerary _____ 137
Art and Culture Itinerary _____ 140
Romantic Itinerary _____ 144
Food and Wine Itinerary _____ 149
Historical Itinerary _____ 152
Outdoor Adventure Itinerary _____ 156

Conclusion _____ *163*

Disclaimer: Kindly Read This Notice Before You Continue

Step into the pages of this travel guide and prepare for a truly extraordinary experience. Delve into the captivating world of Dominican Republic where imagination, creativity, and a thirst for adventure reign supreme. You won't find any images within these pages, as we firmly believe in the power of firsthand exploration, devoid of visual filters or preconceptions. Each monument, every nook and cranny eagerly awaits your arrival, ready to astonish and amaze. Why spoil the thrill of that initial glimpse, that overwhelming sense of wonder? So get ready to embark on an unparalleled journey, where your imagination becomes the sole means of transportation and you, the ultimate guide. Release any preconceived notions and allow yourself to be transported to an authentic Dominican Republic experience brimming with hidden treasures. Let the enchantment commence, but remember, the most breathtaking images will be the ones painted by your own eyes.

Unlike many conventional guides, this book needs no detailed maps. Why, you may ask? Because we firmly believe that the truest discoveries happen when you wander, when you surrender to the current of the surroundings and embrace the uncertainty of the path. No rigid itineraries or precise directions are provided here, for we yearn for you to explore Dominican Republic on your own terms, unbound by limitations or restrictions. Surrender yourself to the currents and unearth hidden gems that no map could reveal. Be audacious, follow your instincts, and brace yourself for serendipitous encounters. The magic of the journey commences now, within a world without maps, where roads materialize with each step and the most extraordinary adventures await in the folds of the unknown.

Chapter 1: Introduction to the Dominican Republic

The Dominican Republic: a jewel in the heart of the Caribbean, where vibrant culture meets pristine beaches, and adventure beckons at every turn. Welcome to a land of boundless possibilities, where every moment is an opportunity to create memories that will last a lifetime.

In "55+ Fun and Cool Things to Do in and around the Dominican Republic," we embark on a journey to uncover the hidden treasures and well-known wonders of this enchanting nation. From the sun-soaked shores of Punta Cana to the historical riches of Santo Domingo's Zona Colonial, this book is your passport to an extraordinary adventure.

Imagine yourself lounging on the silky sands of Bahia de las Aguilas, the gentle caress of the Caribbean breeze whispering secrets of ancient shores. Picture the rush of exhilaration as you soar through the treetops on a zip-line in the Anamuya Mountains, or the quiet awe that washes over you in the presence of the Taino Caves' timeless mysteries.

Savor the rich flavors of Mangu, experience the comforting embrace of Mofongo, and delve into the tantalizing world of Dominican coffee. From street food in Santiago to chocolate-making workshops in Puerto Plata, every dish tells a story, and you're invited to partake in this delectable narrative.

Dance to the infectious rhythms of Merengue and Bachata, explore the depths of the Larimar mines in Barahona, and witness the artistry of Dominican cigars being hand-rolled in time-honored tradition. Engage with the vibrant tapestry of Dominican culture, and let it leave an indelible mark on your soul.

Embark on heart-pounding adventures, from conquering the heights of Pico Duarte, the Caribbean's tallest peak, to exploring the depths of Los Haitises National Park's ancient caves. Dive into the crystal-clear waters of Bayahibe's coral reefs or witness the majestic grace of humpback whales in Samaná.

Indulge in spa retreats that rejuvenate both body and soul, partake in yoga and meditation sessions against the backdrop of Las Galeras' serene beauty, and experience the natural healing properties of La Ciénaga's hot springs. Let go of the ordinary and embrace the extraordinary.

In this book, we've curated a selection of 55 experiences that will introduce you to the heartbeat of the Dominican Republic. Whether you're an intrepid explorer, a culture enthusiast, a food lover, or simply seeking a slice of paradise, there's something here for everyone.

So, fasten your seatbelt and prepare to be swept away by the magic of the Dominican Republic. Let these pages be your guide, and let the adventures begin!

Overview of the Country

The Dominican Republic, often referred to as the "DR," is a captivating Caribbean nation known for its rich cultural heritage, stunning landscapes, and warm hospitality. Situated on the eastern two-thirds of the island of Hispaniola, it shares its western border with Haiti. This tropical paradise boasts a diverse topography, ranging from pristine beaches along its extensive coastline to lush, mountainous interiors.

The DR is a land of geographical contrasts. The fertile Cibao Valley in the north is known as the country's breadbasket, with rolling hills and fertile plains producing a bounty of agricultural products. In stark contrast, the southwest is characterized by arid deserts and cacti-studded landscapes.

With a history deeply intertwined with both indigenous Taino culture and Spanish colonial influence, the Dominican Republic offers a unique blend of traditions. Visitors are often struck by the rhythm of Merengue music, the zest for life displayed in colorful celebrations, and the warm smiles of locals.

Language and Cuisine
Spanish is the official language, though English is widely understood in tourist areas. The cuisine is a tantalizing fusion of Spanish, African, and Taino flavors. Staples like mangu (mashed plantains) and mofongo (fried plantains with garlic and meat) offer a delicious taste of the local culture.

Economic Hub of the Caribbean
Beyond its natural beauty, the Dominican Republic boasts a growing economy, fueled by agriculture, tourism, and a burgeoning manufacturing sector. Its strategic location in the Caribbean has also made it an attractive destination for international trade.

Tourism at its Heart
Tourism is a cornerstone of the Dominican economy. Visitors flock to the country for its idyllic beaches, vibrant cities, and a plethora of activities ranging from water sports to cultural experiences. Whether you're seeking relaxation, adventure, or a taste of history, the DR has something to offer every traveler.

1Cultural Insights

The Dominican Republic is a vibrant tapestry of cultures, shaped by a complex history that spans indigenous Taino roots, Spanish colonialism, African heritage, and a touch of modern globalization. Understanding the rich cultural fabric of this nation will greatly enhance your experience as you explore its landscapes and interact with its people.

Taino Legacy and Indigenous Influences
The Taino people, the original inhabitants of the island, have left an indelible mark on Dominican culture. Their legacy is visible in the names of places, such as "Higuey" and "Yamasa," and in the cuisine, with staples like cassava and yams. Traditional Taino ceremonies, like the "areito" dances, still find echoes in modern Dominican festivals.

Colonial Heritage in the Zona Colonial
Santo Domingo's Zona Colonial is a UNESCO World Heritage Site and a living museum of Spanish colonial architecture. Cobblestone streets, towering fortresses, and centuries-old churches transport visitors back to the 16th century. The Alcázar de Colón, once the home of Christopher Columbus' son Diego, offers a window into the opulent lifestyle of Spanish nobility during the colonial era.

African Roots in Music and Dance
The rhythmic heartbeat of the Dominican Republic is found in its music and dance. Influenced by the African diaspora, genres like Merengue and Bachata have evolved into internationally acclaimed styles. Merengue, with its infectious beat, is the national dance, while Bachata, once a music of the rural poor, now graces stages worldwide.

Carnival: A Feast of Colors and Tradition
The Dominican Carnival is a lively and exuberant celebration that takes place throughout February. A fusion of European,

African, and Taino traditions, it's a riot of color, music, and dance. Elaborate costumes, masks, and vibrant parades fill the streets, creating an atmosphere of sheer revelry.

Religion and Spirituality
Catholicism plays a central role in Dominican life, a legacy of Spanish colonization. Churches, from the grandeur of the Basilica de la Altagracia to humble countryside chapels, dot the landscape. Yet, intertwined with Catholicism is a vibrant undercurrent of syncretic spirituality, blending African, Taino, and European elements. This is perhaps most evident in the celebration of "Fiesta de la Virgen de la Altagracia," a religious event infused with indigenous rituals.

Warmth and Hospitality of the Dominican People
One of the most endearing aspects of Dominican culture is the warmth and hospitality of its people. Known for their friendliness and open-heartedness, Dominicans are quick to welcome visitors into their homes and communities. Engaging with locals offers a profound insight into their way of life and the values they hold dear.

By delving into the cultural mosaic of the Dominican Republic, you'll not only gain a deeper appreciation for the country's history but also forge meaningful connections with its people, making your journey all the more enriching and memorable. Embrace the diversity, savor the traditions, and let the vibrant culture of the Dominican Republic leave an indelible mark on your heart.

Getting Around
Navigating the Dominican Republic is an integral part of ensuring a smooth and enjoyable trip. The country offers a range of transportation options to suit different preferences and budgets. Understanding the available choices will help you make the most of your time exploring this vibrant destination.

Rental Cars
Renting a car is a popular choice for travelers who prefer the freedom of exploring at their own pace. Major cities like Santo Domingo, Punta Cana, and Puerto Plata have well-established car rental agencies, offering a diverse selection of vehicles to cater to various needs. Keep in mind that driving in the Dominican Republic follows right-hand traffic rules, similar to the United States.

Before renting a car, make sure to have a valid driver's license and consider purchasing additional insurance coverage, especially if you plan on venturing into rural or less-traveled areas. Be cautious of local driving customs and road conditions, and always follow traffic regulations.

Taxis and Ride-Sharing Services
Taxis are readily available in urban centers and tourist areas. They are a convenient mode of transportation for short distances or when you prefer to avoid the hassle of parking. Ensure the taxi has a working meter, or agree on a fare before beginning your journey.

In recent years, ride-sharing services like Uber and Lyft have gained popularity in some parts of the Dominican Republic, providing an alternative to traditional taxis. These services often offer transparent pricing and the convenience of booking through a mobile app.

Public Transportation
The Dominican Republic has a well-established public transportation system, particularly in larger cities. Buses and minibusses, known as "guaguas," are affordable options for getting around. They operate on designated routes, and schedules may vary. Be sure to check for the latest information on routes and fares.

In Santo Domingo, the Metro system provides a quick and efficient way to travel within the city. It connects key points of interest and neighborhoods, making it a popular choice for both locals and tourists.

Motoconchos and Carritos Públicos
For shorter distances within cities or towns, motoconchos and carritos públicos offer an economical means of transport. Motoconchos are motorcycle taxis, while carritos públicos are shared vans or trucks that follow specific routes. These modes of transportation are widely used by locals and can provide an authentic cultural experience for adventurous travelers.

Domestic Flights
When covering longer distances or traveling between major cities, domestic flights are a time-saving option. The Dominican Republic has a well-connected network of airports, with several carriers offering regular flights between key destinations. This is particularly useful for those wanting to explore both coasts or visit remote areas.

Choosing the right mode of transportation depends on your travel preferences, itinerary, and budget. It's recommended to plan ahead and consider a combination of options to make the most of your time in the Dominican Republic. Whether you opt for the convenience of a rental car, the affordability of public transportation, or the thrill of a motoconcho ride, getting around in this diverse country is an adventure in itself

Chapter 2: Beach Adventures

Relaxing on Punta Cana Beach

Nestled along the eastern coast of the Dominican Republic, Punta Cana Beach stands as a testament to the Caribbean's unrivaled beauty. With its powdery white sands and crystal-clear turquoise waters, it's no wonder why this stretch of shoreline has earned a reputation as one of the world's premier beach destinations.

A Tropical Paradise
As you step onto the beach, a gentle breeze carries the scent of saltwater and the soothing rhythm of waves fills the air. The first thing that strikes you is the powdery texture of the sand, soft and cool beneath your feet. The sand here is renowned for its fine grain, making it ideal for lounging, building sandcastles, or taking leisurely strolls along the shore.

Turquoise Waters and Water Sports
The waters of Punta Cana Beach beckon with their mesmerizing shades of blue and green. They're remarkably clear, allowing you to see the colorful marine life swimming beneath the surface. Whether you're a seasoned snorkeler or a first-timer, the coral reefs just offshore offer an underwater spectacle that's not to be missed.

For those seeking a bit more adventure, Punta Cana offers an array of water sports. You can try your hand at windsurfing, paddleboarding, or even embark on a thrilling jet ski ride. The calm, protected bay makes it an excellent spot for beginners, while experienced water enthusiasts can venture farther out for a more exhilarating experience.

Serenity and Seclusion
Despite its popularity, Punta Cana Beach manages to exude an air of tranquility. While there are resorts and amenities nearby, there are also secluded spots where you can carve out your own private slice of paradise. Settle into a hammock strung between two palm trees, or lay out on a beach towel under the shade of an umbrella.

Beachfront Cuisine and Refreshments
The beach is dotted with charming beach bars and restaurants, offering a tantalizing array of local and international cuisine. From freshly caught seafood to tropical fruit platters, the culinary offerings complement the natural splendor of the surroundings. Sip on a refreshing coconut water or indulge in a frosty piña colada as you soak in the sun and sea.

Sunset Magic
As the day winds down, Punta Cana Beach transforms into a canvas of warm, golden hues. The setting sun paints the sky with fiery reds and oranges, casting a serene glow over the landscape. It's a moment that feels almost surreal, a reminder of nature's ability to inspire awe and wonder.

Exploring Bahia de las Aguilas
Nestled along the southwestern coast of the Dominican Republic lies the untouched paradise of Bahia de las Aguilas. This pristine stretch of coastline, often referred to as the "Eagles' Bay," is a testament to nature's unspoiled beauty and a testament to the Dominican Republic's commitment to preserving its natural wonders.

A Natural Haven
Bahia de las Aguilas is not your typical beach destination. Accessible only by boat or a rugged trek through the Jaragua National Park, this secluded bay is a haven for those seeking

a true escape from the hustle and bustle of modern life. The journey to reach this hidden gem is an adventure in itself, leading through dense coastal vegetation, across mangrove forests, and over limestone formations.

Turquoise Waters and Powder-Soft Sand
Upon arrival, visitors are greeted by a breathtaking sight. The bay boasts some of the clearest, most turquoise waters in the Caribbean. The gentle lapping of waves against the shore creates a soothing soundtrack, inviting visitors to unwind and connect with nature. The powdery, white sand stretches for miles, providing ample space for both relaxation and exploration.

Snorkeling and Marine Marvels
Beyond its stunning shorelines, Bahia de las Aguilas offers an underwater wonderland for snorkeling enthusiasts. The coral reefs that fringe the bay are teeming with an array of marine life. Colorful fish dart amongst the corals, creating a mesmerizing display of biodiversity. Snorkelers can also encounter graceful sea turtles and, if lucky, even playful dolphins that occasionally grace the bay with their presence.

Exploring the Coastal Caves
One of the unique features of Bahia de las Aguilas is the presence of coastal caves carved into the limestone cliffs that border the beach. These caves, formed over millennia by the erosive forces of wind and water, offer a fascinating glimpse into the geological history of the region. Explorers can wander through the cool, dimly lit interiors, marveling at the intricate patterns etched by nature.

Preservation and Conservation Efforts
Bahia de las Aguilas owes its pristine condition to a combination of strict conservation efforts and limited access. The Dominican government, along with environmental

organizations, has taken great strides to protect this natural wonder. Strict regulations limit the number of visitors allowed at any given time, ensuring that the bay's delicate ecosystem remains undisturbed.

Sunset Serenity
As the day draws to a close, Bahia de las Aguilas offers a magical sunset experience. The horizon transforms into a canvas of warm hues, casting a golden glow over the bay. Visitors often find a quiet spot along the shore to witness this awe-inspiring spectacle, a moment of serenity that leaves an indelible mark on the soul.

In the heart of Bahia de las Aguilas, time seems to stand still. It's a place where the rhythms of nature take precedence, and where the demands of the modern world fade away. For those fortunate enough to experience its wonders, Bahia de las Aguilas remains a cherished memory, a testament to the enduring beauty of the Dominican Republic's natural landscapes.

Kite Surfing in Cabarete

Nestled along the northern coast of the Dominican Republic lies a paradise for water sports enthusiasts - Cabarete. This coastal town, with its steady trade winds and azure waters, has gained international acclaim as one of the premier destinations for kite surfing.

A Mecca for Kite Surfers
Cabarete's reputation as a mecca for kite surfing is well-deserved. The unique geographical layout of the bay, coupled with consistent trade winds, creates the perfect conditions for kite surfing. As the sun kisses the horizon, the bay comes alive with colorful kites, their silhouettes dancing against the backdrop of a fiery sky.

Ideal Conditions for All Skill Levels

One of the remarkable aspects of Cabarete is its inclusivity. Whether you're a seasoned kite surfer or a novice eager to learn, Cabarete offers something for everyone. The bay is spacious, providing ample room for both beginners to practice their skills and advanced riders to push their limits.

For beginners, there are numerous kite schools along the beach, staffed by certified instructors who prioritize safety and skill development. These professionals offer patient guidance, ensuring newcomers to the sport can progress at their own pace.

The Wind that Beckons

The wind in Cabarete is a faithful companion to kite surfers. From June to September, the trade winds sweep consistently across the bay, providing optimal conditions for riders. During this period, the wind speed typically ranges from 15 to 25 knots, creating a thrilling playground for kite surfers to harness its energy.

For those seeking a more tranquil experience, the months of October to May offer lighter winds, making it an ideal time for beginners and freestyle enthusiasts. The bay transforms into a serene oasis, where riders can hone their skills or simply revel in the beauty of the surroundings.

Beyond the Waves

Kite surfing in Cabarete is not only about adrenaline-pumping action on the water. The vibrant kite surfing community adds a unique dimension to the experience. The camaraderie among riders, both local and international, fosters an atmosphere of shared passion and mutual respect.

In the evenings, the town of Cabarete comes to life with a bustling nightlife. From beachfront bars to quaint restaurants, there's no shortage of places to unwind and relive the day's adventures. Live music fills the air, providing the perfect soundtrack to a day of exhilarating rides and salty sea breezes.

Safety First
Safety is paramount in Cabarete's kite surfing culture. Local authorities and kite schools work tirelessly to ensure that safety guidelines are followed. Riders are encouraged to wear appropriate safety gear, undergo proper training, and adhere to established protocols.

In Cabarete, kite surfing is more than just a sport; it's a way of life. The marriage of wind and waves in this coastal haven creates an environment where riders of all levels can thrive. Whether you seek the rush of catching air or the serenity of gliding across calm waters, Cabarete invites you to experience the magic of kite surfing. So, grab your board and harness the wind - adventure awaits in Cabarete!

Snorkeling in Saona Island
Saona Island, a gem of the Dominican Republic, beckons with its crystalline waters and abundant marine life. Snorkeling here is a journey into a world of vibrant coral reefs, playful fish, and underwater wonders that captivate the senses.

The Underwater Paradise
As you dip beneath the surface, you'll be greeted by a kaleidoscope of colors. The coral gardens stretch out like a living tapestry, swaying gently with the ebb and flow of the tide. Soft corals, in hues of pink, purple, and orange, wave in rhythm with the ocean's dance.

The Marine Residents

Saona Island is home to a diverse community of marine creatures. Schools of tropical fish, like vibrant parrotfish and curious angelfish, dart among the corals, their scales flashing in the dappled sunlight. Keep an eye out for elusive seahorses nestled in the nooks and crannies, and graceful sea turtles gliding through the water with an air of ancient wisdom.

The Coral Gardens
The coral reefs themselves are a masterpiece of nature's engineering. Delicate branching corals provide shelter for tiny crustaceans, while massive brain corals create intricate mazes for small fish to dart through. Fan corals sway with the gentle current, creating a mesmerizing display of movement.

Snorkeling Spots
Saona Island offers a variety of snorkeling spots, each with its own unique charm. The Catuano Reef, in the island's vicinity, is a popular choice for snorkelers. Here, the shallow waters make it easy for beginners to explore, while still offering a wealth of marine life to discover.

Conservation Efforts
Preserving the delicate balance of Saona Island's marine ecosystem is of paramount importance. Local initiatives and conservation organizations work tirelessly to protect the reefs from pollution and over-tourism. Responsible snorkeling practices, such as refraining from touching or standing on the corals, are strongly encouraged to ensure that future generations can continue to enjoy this underwater paradise.

Tips for a Memorable Snorkeling Experience

- Choose the Right Gear: A well-fitting mask, snorkel, and fins are essential for a comfortable and enjoyable experience.

- Practice Proper Buoyancy: Avoid touching or standing on the coral reefs, as this can cause irreparable damage.

- Respect Wildlife: Observe marine life from a respectful distance and refrain from attempting to touch or chase after them.

- Use Eco-Friendly Sunscreen: Opt for reef-safe sunscreen to protect both your skin and the delicate underwater environment.

- Follow Local Guidelines: Listen to your snorkeling guide and adhere to any specific instructions they provide for a safe and enjoyable experience.

Snorkeling in Saona Island is a transformative experience that allows you to step into a world of unparalleled beauty and diversity. As you glide through the water, you become a guest in a realm that has been flourishing for millennia. By embracing responsible snorkeling practices, you can play a vital role in preserving this underwater paradise for generations to come.

Beachcombing in Bahia de las Calderas

Nestled along the southwestern coast of the Dominican Republic lies the picturesque Bahia de las Calderas, a hidden gem for beachcombers and nature enthusiasts alike. Known for its pristine beaches, crystal-clear waters, and rich biodiversity, this coastal paradise offers a unique experience for those seeking to uncover the secrets of the Caribbean shores.

A Beachcomber's Paradise
Bahia de las Calderas boasts an extensive stretch of coastline, characterized by powdery white sands and gentle turquoise waves. The beachcombing opportunities here are unparalleled, with an abundance of treasures waiting to be discovered at the water's edge. Seashells of various shapes and sizes, colorful sea glass, and intricately patterned coral fragments are just a few of the delights that wash ashore, offering a glimpse into the vibrant marine life thriving beneath the surface.

The Art of Beachcombing
Beachcombing is not merely a pastime; it's an art form. It requires a keen eye, patience, and a profound appreciation for the beauty that nature bestows upon the shore. As you wander along the beach, the rhythmic sound of waves serves as a soothing backdrop, creating a serene ambiance that heightens the experience. Each step unveils a new possibility, a hidden treasure waiting to be discovered.

Seashells Galore
One of the most enchanting aspects of beachcombing in Bahia de las Calderas is the diverse array of seashells that adorn the sands. Conch shells, with their spiral intricacies, tell tales of the creatures that once called them home. Scallop shells, delicate and symmetrical, glisten in the sunlight, offering a glimpse into the precision of nature's craftsmanship. The occasional rare find, such as a perfectly intact sand dollar, becomes a cherished keepsake, a tangible memory of a day spent in harmony with the sea.

Sea Glass Treasures

Sea glass, nature's own form of recycled art, is another prized discovery for beachcombers. Smoothed and frosted by years of tumbling in the waves, these colorful fragments of glass tell stories of maritime history. From cobalt blues to emerald greens, each piece carries a unique aura, a testament to the transformative power of the ocean.

Coral Creations

The remnants of coral colonies, delicately shaped and etched by the sea's caress, add a touch of natural elegance to the beachcombing experience. Intricate patterns and vibrant hues hint at the underwater world that lies just beyond the shoreline. These coral fragments, once part of thriving reef ecosystems, now find new purpose as cherished souvenirs, evoking a sense of wonder and reverence for the sea's boundless beauty.

Conservation and Respect

While beachcombing in Bahia de las Calderas is a delightful pursuit, it is essential to approach it with a spirit of conservation and respect for the environment. Leave only footprints, taking care not to disturb fragile ecosystems or disturb nesting sites. By appreciating the natural wonders of the beach without causing harm, we ensure that future generations can also revel in the magic of this coastal haven.

In Bahia de las Calderas, beachcombing becomes a journey of connection - to the sea, to nature, and to the timeless beauty that washes ashore with each gentle wave. As you explore this coastal sanctuary, let the whispers of the sea guide your steps, and may you leave with treasures that forever remind you of the enchantment that awaits along the shores of the Dominican Republic.

Chapter 3: Historical Marvels

Visiting the Zona Colonial in Santo Domingo

Nestled along the azure coastline of the Caribbean Sea, the Zona Colonial in Santo Domingo stands as a living testament to the rich history and cultural heritage of the Dominican Republic. This UNESCO World Heritage Site is a treasure trove of colonial architecture, cobbled streets, and centuries-old landmarks, offering visitors a captivating journey back in time.

A Glimpse into the Past
As you step into the Zona Colonial, you are immediately enveloped in an atmosphere of old-world charm. The streets, lined with well-preserved colonial buildings, echo with stories of conquests, trade, and cultural exchange. This historic quarter, founded in 1498 by Bartholomew Columbus, the younger brother of Christopher Columbus, is the oldest European settlement in the Americas.

Architectural Marvels
One of the most striking features of the Zona Colonial is its architectural diversity. Walking along Calle Las Damas, the first paved street in the New World, you'll encounter a captivating blend of Gothic, Moorish, and Renaissance styles. The Catedral Primada de América, the first cathedral in the Americas, with its coral limestone façade, stands as a prominent example of 16th-century Spanish architecture. Nearby, the Alcazar de Colón, once the residence of Christopher Columbus' son, Diego, offers a glimpse into the opulent lifestyle of the colonial elite.

Cobblestone Streets and Plazas
Meandering through the Zona Colonial, the cobblestone streets lead you to charming plazas, each with its own unique character. Parque Colon, named after Christopher Columbus, serves as a central gathering point. Here, locals and tourists alike gather to soak in the vibrant atmosphere, with artists, musicians, and street vendors contributing to the lively ambiance.

Museums and Cultural Institutions
For those eager to delve deeper into the history and culture of the Dominican Republic, the Zona Colonial is home to an array of museums and cultural institutions. The Museo de las Casas Reales, housed in a grand colonial building, offers a comprehensive look at the colonial period through an extensive collection of artifacts and exhibits. The Museo del Ámbar showcases the country's rich reserves of amber, a fossilized resin highly valued for its intricate inclusions.

Culinary Delights and Local Flavors
The Zona Colonial is not only a haven for history enthusiasts but also a paradise for food lovers. Cafés and restaurants tucked away in colonial courtyards serve up a delightful array of local and international cuisine. From traditional mangu for breakfast to succulent mofongo for dinner, the culinary offerings reflect the vibrant blend of cultures that have shaped Dominican gastronomy.

Evening Strolls and Cultural Events
As the sun sets over the Caribbean horizon, the Zona Colonial takes on a new, enchanting character. The warm glow of streetlights illuminates the cobbled streets, casting shadows on the facades of historic buildings. Many evenings, you can catch live music performances or open-air cultural

events in the plazas, providing a captivating sensory experience.

Visiting the Zona Colonial in Santo Domingo is not just a journey through history; it's an immersion into the soul of the Dominican Republic. Every cobblestone, every archway, and every bustling plaza tells a story, inviting you to be a part of this living tapestry of culture and heritage. It's a place where the past seamlessly blends with the present, offering an experience that lingers in the hearts of visitors long after they depart.

Discovering the Ruins of Altos de Chavón

Nestled along the picturesque Chavón River, Altos de Chavón stands as a captivating testament to the rich history and artistic legacy of the Dominican Republic. This meticulously recreated 16th-century Mediterranean village transports visitors back in time, offering a glimpse into a bygone era.

A Journey Through Time
As you step onto the cobblestone streets of Altos de Chavón, you'll feel a palpable sense of history. Each stone, each building, whispers tales of artisans and craftsmen who painstakingly constructed this village. The architecture, with its stone façades and arched doorways, mirrors the charming villages of southern Europe.

The Artistic Heartbeat
One of the most enchanting aspects of Altos de Chavón is its thriving artistic community. Artisans and craftsmen, both local and international, come here to hone their skills and find inspiration amidst this cultural haven. The village boasts an art school affiliated with the esteemed Parsons School of

Design in New York, drawing talented students from around the globe.

Views That Inspire
Perched high above the Chavón River, Altos de Chavón offers breathtaking panoramic views of the surrounding landscape. The river winds its way through lush greenery, providing a picturesque backdrop that has inspired countless artists and filmmakers.

The Amphitheater: A Stage for Legends
At the heart of Altos de Chavón lies an open-air amphitheater, an enchanting venue that has hosted world-renowned artists. With its stone seating and unparalleled acoustics, the amphitheater creates a truly magical setting for concerts and events. As the sun sets, the amphitheater comes alive with music, casting a spell on all who are fortunate enough to be in attendance.

The Museo Arqueológico Regional
For history enthusiasts, a visit to the Museo Arqueológico Regional is a must. This regional archaeological museum houses an impressive collection of artifacts, shedding light on the pre-Columbian Taino culture that once thrived in the Dominican Republic. From intricately crafted pottery to ceremonial objects, each piece tells a compelling story of a civilization that predates the arrival of the Europeans.

Culinary Delights and Artisan Boutiques
Altos de Chavón also offers a delightful array of dining options and boutique shops. Whether you're savoring traditional Dominican cuisine or browsing handcrafted jewelry and art, every corner of this village exudes a unique charm.

Sunset Serenity

As the day draws to a close, Altos de Chavón takes on a serene and ethereal quality. The golden hues of the setting sun cast long shadows over the cobblestone streets, creating a tranquil atmosphere that invites quiet contemplation.

In the heart of Altos de Chavón, time seems to stand still. Whether you're an art enthusiast, a history buff, or simply a traveler in search of a truly unique experience, this village offers something for everyone. With its timeless beauty and cultural richness, Altos de Chavón is a place where the past and the present converge in perfect harmony.

Exploring Fort San Felipe in Puerto Plata

Perched majestically on a rocky promontory overlooking the azure waters of the Atlantic Ocean, Fort San Felipe stands as a sentinel of history in Puerto Plata, Dominican Republic. This formidable structure, named after King Philip II of Spain, is a testament to the strategic importance of Puerto Plata in the colonial era.

Historical Significance
Built in the late 16th century, Fort San Felipe was commissioned by King Philip II to defend against the ever-present threat of pirates and privateers that plagued the Caribbean during that time. Its strategic location at the entrance of the Bay of Puerto Plata made it a crucial defense for the Spanish settlers against marauding buccaneers.

Architectural Grandeur
The fort's architecture is a striking blend of Spanish military engineering and Caribbean practicality. Its solid stone walls, constructed from local coral stone, rise imposingly from the cliffs, creating an awe-inspiring silhouette against the skyline. The layout, characterized by a pentagonal shape, is a

marvel of medieval military design, allowing for a wide field of fire and excellent vantage points.

Museum and Exhibits

Today, Fort San Felipe has been meticulously restored and transformed into a captivating museum. As visitors step through its weathered gates, they are transported back in time. The museum's exhibits chronicle the rich history of Puerto Plata, delving into the lives of the soldiers who once stood guard here and the turbulent times they lived in. Artefacts such as weaponry, uniforms, and navigational instruments are on display, offering a tangible connection to the past.

Panoramic Views

One of the most enchanting aspects of Fort San Felipe is its panoramic view. From the battlements, visitors are treated to a breathtaking vista of Puerto Plata, with its vibrant pastel-colored houses, swaying palm trees, and the shimmering ocean beyond. It's a picture-perfect scene that captures the essence of the Caribbean.

Interactive Experiences

For those with a thirst for interactive experiences, the fort offers a range of activities. Guided tours led by knowledgeable historians provide in-depth insights into the fort's history and its role in the Caribbean's colonial struggles. Additionally, there are reenactments of historical events, allowing visitors to step into the shoes of the soldiers who once defended this bastion.

Practical Information

Location: Fort San Felipe is located at the northernmost point of the Malecón, Puerto Plata's seafront promenade.
Opening Hours: The fort is open to visitors from 9:00 AM to 5:00 PM, seven days a week.
Admission: The entrance fee is modest, making it an accessible attraction for travelers of all budgets.

Visiting Fort San Felipe is a journey through time, a chance to immerse oneself in the legacy of a bygone era. Its evocative walls whisper tales of conquests, sieges, and the resilient spirit of those who called it home. For anyone with an interest in history or a love for captivating vistas, a visit to Fort San Felipe is an absolute must when exploring Puerto Plata.

El Faro Lighthouse in Punta Rucia

Perched majestically on the rugged cliffs of Punta Rucia, the El Faro Lighthouse stands as a silent sentinel, overseeing the turquoise waters of the Atlantic Ocean. This historic landmark is not only a testament to the Dominican Republic's rich maritime heritage but also offers visitors a breathtaking panoramic view of the surrounding coastline.

History and Significance
The El Faro Lighthouse, whose name translates to "The Lighthouse" in Spanish, has a storied history dating back to the early 19th century. Originally constructed in 1868 by Spanish engineers, it was built to guide ships safely through the treacherous waters of the Atlantic, ensuring their safe passage to and from the nearby ports.

Over the years, the lighthouse has weathered storms, witnessed historical events, and played a crucial role in the region's maritime trade. Its enduring presence stands as a testament to the resilience and craftsmanship of the builders who constructed it.

Architectural Marvel
The lighthouse is a fine example of neoclassical architecture, characterized by its elegant proportions and graceful symmetry. Standing at an impressive height of 54 meters (177 feet), it commands attention with its whitewashed facade that gleams brilliantly under the Caribbean sun. The

tower is adorned with intricate ironwork and a distinctive lantern room that houses the powerful beacon.

The Lure of the View
Visitors who venture to the El Faro Lighthouse are rewarded with one of the most awe-inspiring vistas in the Dominican Republic. From the observation deck, which is accessible via a spiraling staircase, a sweeping panorama unfolds before your eyes. To the east, the azure waters stretch endlessly, merging with the horizon in a harmonious display of nature's grandeur. To the west, the coastline reveals hidden coves, pristine beaches, and the verdant hills that cradle Punta Rucia.

Preservation Efforts
In recent years, concerted efforts have been made to preserve and restore this historic gem. Preservationists have worked diligently to maintain the lighthouse's structural integrity, ensuring that it continues to stand proudly for generations to come. The surrounding grounds have been landscaped, providing a welcoming environment for visitors while preserving the natural beauty of the area.

Visitor Experience
A visit to the El Faro Lighthouse is not only a journey through history but also an opportunity for contemplation and connection with nature. As the gentle sea breeze carries the scent of saltwater, visitors can take in the sight and sound of waves crashing against the cliffs, immersing themselves in the timeless rhythm of the ocean.

The El Faro Lighthouse in Punta Rucia is more than a navigational aid; it is a living testament to the enduring spirit of the Dominican Republic. Its towering presence, coupled with the breathtaking views it offers, make it a must-visit destination for travelers seeking a blend of history, natural beauty, and maritime wonder. Standing on the edge of the cliffs, one can't help but be moved by the legacy of this iconic structure, which continues to illuminate both the seas and the hearts of those who behold it.

Taino Caves in Los Haitises National Park

Deep within the heart of the Dominican Republic lies a hidden treasure trove of history and natural beauty - the Taino Caves in Los Haitises National Park. These ancient caves, etched into the limestone cliffs, offer a fascinating glimpse into the rich cultural heritage of the Taino people, the indigenous inhabitants of the Caribbean. Visiting these caves is like stepping back in time, immersing oneself in a world where art and spirituality converged in the most captivating way.

A Window to the Past
The Taino Caves, nestled amidst the lush greenery of Los Haitises, hold a significant place in the history of the Dominican Republic. The Taino people, skilled artisans and farmers, adorned these caves with intricate petroglyphs and pictographs that depict scenes from their daily lives, cosmology, and spiritual beliefs. These ancient artworks, some dating back over a thousand years, offer invaluable insights into the Taino's customs, rituals, and artistic expressions.

The Artistic Marvels
Upon entering the caves, visitors are greeted by a mesmerizing array of symbols and figures. Abstract designs intertwine with representations of animals, celestial bodies, and human forms. The skill and artistry of the Taino people are evident in every stroke, revealing a deep connection between the natural world and their spiritual beliefs.

One notable cave, known as "Cueva de la Línea," features a striking petroglyph panel that portrays various human figures, celestial bodies, and geometric shapes. Each element carries its own significance, offering tantalizing clues about the Taino's cosmological beliefs and societal structure.

Spiritual Significance
For the Taino, these caves held profound spiritual significance. They were considered sacred spaces, where rituals, ceremonies, and gatherings took place. The echoes of these ancient practices still reverberate through the cool, damp air, creating an aura of reverence that is palpable to modern-day visitors.

Exploring the Caves
Exploring the Taino Caves is an adventure in itself. Guided tours, led by knowledgeable local guides, navigate through the labyrinthine passages, shedding light on the history, art, and cultural significance of these ancient spaces. As you traverse the dimly lit chambers, it's easy to imagine the flickering light of torches illuminating the walls as the Taino people created their masterpieces.

Preserving a Legacy
Preserving the Taino Caves and the cultural heritage they represent is of paramount importance. Conservation efforts are underway to protect these sacred spaces from natural erosion and human impact. Visitors are encouraged to treat these caves with the utmost respect, leaving no trace of their passage.

A visit to the Taino Caves in Los Haitises National Park is a journey into the heart of Dominican history and culture. It's an opportunity to connect with the ancient souls who once inhabited this land, leaving behind a legacy etched in stone.

As you stand in the presence of these awe-inspiring artworks, you can't help but feel a profound sense of gratitude for the opportunity to witness and preserve this invaluable piece of human history.

Chapter 4: Outdoor Adventures

Hiking Pico Duarte, the Caribbean's Highest Peak

Nestled in the heart of the Dominican Republic, Pico Duarte stands as an emblematic peak, inviting intrepid adventurers to embark on a journey that promises both challenge and awe-inspiring beauty. Rising majestically to an elevation of 3,098 meters (10,164 feet) above sea level, Pico Duarte not only reigns as the highest summit in the Caribbean but also offers a trek through some of the most breathtaking landscapes the island nation has to offer.

The Trailhead and Preparations

The adventure begins at the trailhead located in the town of Jarabacoa, where eager hikers gather to prepare for the ascent. It's crucial to start early in the day to maximize daylight hours and allow ample time for the climb. A seasoned guide is highly recommended, as they bring invaluable knowledge of the terrain, weather patterns, and essential safety precautions.

The Ascension: A Glimpse into Diverse Ecosystems

The ascent of Pico Duarte takes hikers on a remarkable journey through diverse ecological zones. The lower slopes are cloaked in lush, tropical rainforests, resplendent with an array of flora and fauna. As one ascends, the landscape gradually shifts, revealing pine forests and alpine meadows, reminiscent of scenes from a storybook.

The Enchanting Cloud Forests

Around the halfway mark, hikers are greeted by the ethereal beauty of cloud forests. Here, mist shrouds the surroundings, creating an almost mystical ambiance. Giant tree ferns and moss-covered rocks add to the enchantment, while the calls of exotic bird species echo through the canopy.

Base Camp: A Respite for Weary Travelers

Approximately halfway through the trek, hikers arrive at Base Camp, a welcome sight for those seeking rest and sustenance. Here, basic accommodations are available, allowing tired adventurers to recharge before pushing onward to the summit. The camaraderie amongst fellow trekkers and the hearty, home-cooked meals prepared by local guides make for a memorable experience.

Summiting Pico Duarte: The Ultimate Reward

The final leg of the journey is the most demanding, requiring determination and resilience. As hikers near the summit, the terrain becomes rocky and steep, demanding careful navigation. Upon reaching the pinnacle, a profound sense of accomplishment washes over, rivaling the panoramic views that stretch across the Dominican landscape. On clear days, the azure expanse of the Caribbean Sea can be seen in the distance, a reminder of the incredible feat achieved.

Reflections and Memories

Descending from Pico Duarte, trekkers carry with them not only a sense of triumph but also a profound connection to the natural beauty and rugged terrain of the Dominican Republic. The memories forged during this epic journey are sure to linger, a testament to the indomitable spirit of adventure that beckons explorers to conquer the Caribbean's highest peak.

Zip-Lining in the Anamuya Mountains

Nestled amidst the lush landscapes of the Dominican Republic, the Anamuya Mountains offer an exhilarating zip-lining experience that promises to leave adventure-seekers awe-inspired. This adrenaline-pumping activity allows you to soar through the treetops, providing a bird's eye view of the pristine tropical rainforest below.

The Thrill of Flight
As you embark on this zip-lining adventure, you'll find yourself at a launch platform perched high above the forest floor. A seasoned guide will expertly outfit you with a secure harness and provide a thorough safety briefing, ensuring that you're well-prepared for the thrilling journey ahead.

With a heart pounding in anticipation, you take that first step onto the platform, and suddenly, you're off. The sensation of wind rushing past, combined with the breathtaking scenery, creates an unparalleled sense of freedom and excitement. The zip-line's cable propels you effortlessly, allowing you to glide through the air like a modern-day Tarzan.

Immersed in Nature's Beauty
As you zip from one platform to the next, you're granted a unique perspective of the Anamuya Mountains' rich biodiversity. Towering trees, cascading waterfalls, and vibrant flora surround you, providing a vivid snapshot of the Dominican Republic's natural splendor.

The forest's soundtrack, a symphony of chirping birds and rustling leaves, underscores the immersive experience. It's a rare opportunity to connect with nature on such an intimate level, as you become a fleeting visitor in this untamed wilderness.

A Series of Adrenaline-Packed Runs
The zip-lining course in the Anamuya Mountains is thoughtfully designed to offer a variety of runs, each with its own unique characteristics. Some lines stretch over vast canyons, while others skim treetops, providing an ever-changing panorama.

The course is meticulously maintained, with safety as the top priority. The guides are trained professionals, adept at ensuring a secure and enjoyable experience for every participant. This means you can focus on relishing the adventure without any concerns about safety.

A Memorable Group Experience
Zip-lining in the Anamuya Mountains is not only a solo adventure; it's also an excellent group activity. Sharing the thrill with friends or family adds an extra layer of enjoyment. The shared moments of excitement and awe as you conquer each run create lasting memories that you'll cherish for years to come.

Zip-lining in the Anamuya Mountains is a quintessential Dominican Republic adventure, offering an unmatched blend of adrenaline, natural beauty, and camaraderie. It's an experience that transcends the ordinary, leaving you with a newfound appreciation for the wonders of the Caribbean's wild heart. Whether you're a seasoned thrill-seeker or a first-time adventurer, this zip-lining escapade promises an unforgettable journey through the treetops of paradise.

White-Water Rafting in Jarabacoa
White-water rafting in Jarabacoa is a thrilling adventure that takes you through some of the most picturesque and

exhilarating rapids in the Dominican Republic. Nestled in the heart of the Central Highlands, Jarabacoa boasts a unique combination of lush rainforests, rugged terrain, and pristine rivers, making it an ideal destination for water-based adventures.

The Experience:
The adventure typically begins with a safety briefing conducted by seasoned guides who are well-versed in the region's topography and the intricacies of navigating the rapids. Participants are provided with the necessary safety gear, including life jackets, helmets, and paddles, and are briefed on essential rafting techniques. Safety is paramount, and guides ensure that everyone is well-prepared before setting out on the river.

The River Yaque del Norte:
The Yaque del Norte River, the longest river in the Dominican Republic, is the primary playground for white-water rafting enthusiasts in Jarabacoa. Its headwaters originate in the Pico Duarte, the highest peak in the Caribbean, and wind their way through Jarabacoa's breathtaking landscape. The river's gradient and varying water flow create an ideal environment for a range of rapids, from gentle ripples to adrenaline-pumping Class III and IV rapids.

The Rapids:
As you embark on this adventure, you'll encounter a series of rapids with evocative names like "El Cerrazo," "La Cienaga," and "El Cajón." Each rapid offers a unique challenge, demanding teamwork and precise paddling techniques to navigate the twists and turns. The rush of adrenaline as you plunge through the waves is nothing short of exhilarating.

The Scenic Beauty:
One of the most enchanting aspects of white-water rafting in Jarabacoa is the opportunity to immerse yourself in the breathtaking natural beauty of the region. Towering trees, vibrant flora, and the distant murmur of waterfalls create a mesmerizing backdrop as you navigate the river. Along the

way, you might catch glimpses of indigenous wildlife, adding an extra layer of excitement to the journey.

Suitable for All Levels:
While white-water rafting in Jarabacoa offers exhilarating challenges for experienced paddlers, it's also accessible to beginners. The river features sections with milder currents, providing a comfortable introduction to this high-energy sport. Guides are adept at tailoring the experience to match the proficiency and comfort level of each group.

Environmental Responsibility:
Operators in Jarabacoa place a strong emphasis on environmental conservation and sustainable tourism practices. They work diligently to minimize the impact of rafting activities on the delicate ecosystem, ensuring that future generations can continue to enjoy this natural wonder.

Horseback Riding in Constanza Valley

Nestled in the heart of the Dominican Republic, the Constanza Valley offers a picturesque landscape that is best explored on horseback. This serene valley, often referred to as the "Switzerland of the Caribbean," is renowned for its lush meadows, verdant hills, and a refreshing climate that provides a perfect setting for an unforgettable horseback riding adventure.

The Experience
Embarking on a horseback riding excursion in Constanza Valley is an immersive experience that allows you to connect with nature in a unique and tranquil way. As you saddle up and begin your journey, you'll be greeted by the gentle clip-clop of your horse's hooves against the earth, creating a soothing rhythm that resonates with the natural surroundings.

Scenic Routes

The valley offers a range of scenic routes, catering to riders of all levels of experience. Novice riders can opt for leisurely trails that wind through rolling meadows, offering breathtaking views of the valley's undulating terrain. For more experienced equestrians, there are challenging paths that ascend into the higher altitudes, providing panoramic vistas of the valley below.

Local Guides

Knowledgeable local guides accompany each excursion, offering insights into the valley's rich history, flora, and fauna. They are intimately familiar with the terrain, ensuring a safe and enjoyable ride for all participants. These guides often share captivating stories about the valley's cultural heritage, making the experience not only visually stunning but intellectually stimulating as well.

Interactions with Wildlife

Horseback riding in Constanza Valley also provides opportunities to encounter the local wildlife. As you traverse the trails, you may catch glimpses of vibrant bird species, including the Hispaniolan Trogon and the Palmchat. The valley is also home to various small mammals and insects, adding an element of natural discovery to your adventure.

Cultural Encounters

In addition to its natural beauty, Constanza Valley is inhabited by warm and welcoming communities. Along the way, riders have the chance to interact with local farmers and artisans, gaining insight into their traditional way of life. This cultural exchange allows for a deeper appreciation of the Dominican Republic's rural heritage.

Practical Considerations
Before embarking on a horseback riding adventure, it's essential to wear comfortable clothing and closed-toe shoes suitable for riding. Helmets are typically provided for safety, and sunscreen is advisable due to the valley's high-altitude exposure.

Caving in Los Haitises National Park

Hidden beneath the lush vegetation and limestone cliffs of Los Haitises National Park lies a captivating underworld of caves and caverns waiting to be explored. This unique geological wonderland, located on the northeastern coast of the Dominican Republic, offers an adventure like no other.

A Subterranean World of Wonders
Los Haitises National Park is renowned for its dramatic karst landscape, characterized by towering cliffs, sinkholes, and underground rivers. Within this natural playground, a network of caves has formed over thousands of years, creating a subterranean world of immense beauty and geological significance.

The Marvels of Cueva del Ángel
One of the park's most celebrated caves is Cueva del Ángel, a cathedral-like chamber adorned with impressive stalactites and stalagmites that have evolved over millennia. As sunlight filters through openings in the cave's ceiling, it illuminates the formations, creating an ethereal atmosphere. The acoustics in this cavern are truly awe-inspiring, leading some to believe it was once used for ceremonial purposes by the indigenous Taino people.

Exploring the Hidden Chambers

Guided tours are available for intrepid explorers keen on unraveling the mysteries of Los Haitises' caves. Equipped with helmets, headlamps, and a sense of wonder, visitors venture deep into the labyrinthine passages. As you navigate through narrow crevices and spacious chambers, you'll encounter otherworldly formations that evoke a sense of both timelessness and constant change.

A Sanctuary for Bats and Wildlife

The caves of Los Haitises serve as sanctuaries for various species of bats, some of which are found nowhere else on the island. These creatures play a vital role in the park's delicate ecosystem, and while exploring, you may catch a glimpse of them in their natural habitat. The eerie yet captivating sounds of their wings fluttering add to the otherworldly ambiance.

Conservation Efforts and Responsible Tourism

Preserving the delicate environment of Los Haitises and its caves is of paramount importance. Visitors are urged to follow strict guidelines to minimize their impact on the fragile ecosystem. This includes refraining from touching formations, avoiding excessive noise, and respecting the natural inhabitants of the caves.

The Spiritual Connection

For many, exploring the caves of Los Haitises is more than just a physical adventure; it's a spiritual journey. The deep, ancient roots of the park and its significance to indigenous cultures provide a profound sense of connection to the natural world and the generations that came before.

Chapter 5: Culinary Delights

Savoring Mangu and Other Traditional Dishes

One of the true pleasures of visiting the Dominican Republic lies in exploring its rich culinary heritage. At the heart of this gastronomic adventure is the beloved dish known as Mangu. A quintessential Dominican breakfast, Mangu is a simple yet deeply satisfying concoction of mashed green plantains, typically served with fried cheese, eggs, and a side of sautéed onions.

The process of making Mangu is an art in itself. Green plantains, chosen for their firmness and subtle sweetness, are peeled, boiled, and then thoroughly mashed until smooth. The result is a creamy, slightly sweet base, which forms the canvas for an array of savory toppings.

Fried cheese, a staple in Dominican cuisine, adds a delightful contrast of textures. Its crisp, golden exterior provides a satisfying crunch, while the inside remains creamy and mild. Paired with the velvety Mangu, it creates a harmonious blend of flavors.

Eggs, prepared to your preference, offer a protein-rich element to the dish. Whether scrambled, sunny-side-up, or poached, they add a comforting familiarity to the plate. The runny yolk of a perfectly cooked egg can even serve as an impromptu sauce, enriching each bite with an extra layer of richness.

To elevate the experience, sautéed onions are a must. Cooked until golden and slightly caramelized, they infuse the dish with a sweet, aromatic essence. Their mellow sweetness counterbalances the savory elements, creating a symphony of flavors that dance on the palate.

Beyond Mangu, the Dominican Republic boasts a treasure trove of traditional dishes. Mofongo, another beloved staple, takes center stage. This dish features mashed fried green plantains mixed with garlic and other seasonings, molded into a mound, and often filled with a choice of meat or seafood. The result is a flavorful explosion of textures and tastes, a true celebration of Dominican culinary expertise.

For those seeking street food adventures, Santiago is the place to be. Here, vibrant food stalls offer a dizzying array of delectable treats. From succulent skewers of grilled meat to empanadas bursting with savory fillings, the options are boundless. Each bite offers a tantalizing glimpse into the dynamic flavors that define Dominican street cuisine.

As you venture through the streets of the Dominican Republic, don't miss out on the opportunity to savor the diverse range of fruits and tropical delights that grace the local markets. From juicy mangoes to creamy avocados, these fruits showcase the vibrant bounty of the island.

Exploring the culinary landscape of the Dominican Republic is a journey that transcends mere sustenance; it's an immersive experience in the culture, history, and vibrant spirit of the island. With every dish, you'll find a story waiting to be told, a tradition waiting to be shared, and a flavor waiting to be savored.

Experiencing the Flavors of Mofongo

When it comes to Dominican cuisine, few dishes are as beloved and iconic as mofongo. This delectable concoction of mashed green plantains, garlic, and crispy pork cracklings is a true representation of the rich and diverse flavors found in Dominican cooking. Whether you're a seasoned food enthusiast or a first-time visitor to the Dominican Republic, indulging in a plate of mofongo is a culinary experience not to be missed.

A Brief History of Mofongo
Mofongo has deep roots in Afro-Dominican culture and can be traced back to West African influences on Caribbean cuisine. The dish evolved over centuries, blending African, Taino, and Spanish culinary traditions. Originally, mofongo was made with yams or yautía, but when plantains became a staple in the Dominican Republic, they quickly became the star ingredient.

Crafting the Perfect Mofongo
Creating an outstanding mofongo requires skill, patience, and an understanding of the delicate balance between textures and flavors. First, ripe green plantains are peeled, sliced, and fried until they achieve a golden crispiness. They are then mashed with garlic, olive oil, and sometimes a splash of broth, resulting in a velvety, aromatic mixture.

The magic of mofongo lies in its versatility. It can be served as a side dish accompanying a main course, or it can take center stage with an array of savory toppings. From succulent shrimp in a garlic sauce to tender chicharrón (fried pork belly) or even a medley of sautéed vegetables, the possibilities are endless.

Regional Variations
While mofongo is a Dominican staple, each region adds its own unique twist. In the south, especially around Santo Domingo, you'll find mofongo dishes that incorporate seafood, reflecting the proximity to the Caribbean Sea. In the

mountainous regions, mofongo is often served with hearty stews and root vegetables, providing comfort and sustenance in cooler climates.

Where to Experience the Best Mofongo
To truly savor the essence of mofongo, venture into local eateries and family-owned restaurants. In Santo Domingo's Zona Colonial, you'll find historic spots that have perfected the art of mofongo over generations. These establishments take pride in sourcing the freshest ingredients and infusing their mofongo with a touch of tradition and a dash of innovation.

Pairing Mofongo with Local Delights
No mofongo experience is complete without a refreshing beverage to complement the flavors. Consider pairing your dish with a chilled Presidente beer, a Dominican favorite, or a tropical fruit juice like passion fruit or guanabana.

The Culmination of Taste and Tradition
In every mouthful of mofongo, you're tasting a fusion of cultures, a celebration of history, and a testament to the culinary artistry of the Dominican people. Whether enjoyed in a bustling city square or a tranquil beachside eatery, mofongo is more than a dish—it's an experience that leaves an indelible mark on your palate and memories.

So, when you find yourself in the Dominican Republic, be sure to seek out this culinary masterpiece. Your taste buds will thank you, and you'll carry with you a piece of Dominican culture that will forever hold a special place in your heart.

Sampling Street Food in Santiago
One of the best ways to experience the local culture is through its street food. The streets of Santiago come alive

with an array of mouthwatering dishes that reflect the fusion of Spanish, African, and Taino influences.

Mangu on the Go

One of the quintessential Dominican breakfast dishes, mangu, can be found at every corner in Santiago. This hearty dish is made from mashed green plantains, served with fried cheese, salami, and often topped with sautéed onions. Vendors take pride in their mangu, each offering their unique twist on this beloved classic.

Pastelón de Plátano Maduro

A close cousin of lasagna, pastelón de plátano maduro is a savory delight. Ripe plantains are layered with seasoned ground meat, cheese, and sometimes black beans, then baked to perfection. The result is a comforting dish with layers of flavors and textures.

Mofongo Stuffed with Chicharrón

Mofongo, a dish originating from Puerto Rico but deeply ingrained in Dominican cuisine, is taken to new heights in Santiago. Here, mofongo is often stuffed with crispy, seasoned chicharrón (fried pork rinds). The contrast of the crispy chicharrón with the garlicky mashed plantains is a taste sensation.

Chimichurri Burger

A Dominican take on the classic burger, the chimichurri burger is a must-try. Juicy, seasoned beef patties are topped with a tangy and flavorful sauce made from mayonnaise, ketchup, and a blend of herbs and spices. Served in a soft bun, it's a handheld delight.

Yuca con Mojo

Yuca, a starchy root vegetable, is a staple in Dominican cuisine. In Santiago, it's often served with a zesty garlic sauce known as mojo. The yuca is boiled to tender perfection and then dressed with the aromatic sauce, creating a simple yet incredibly satisfying dish.

Tips for Street Food Adventures
- Embrace the Local Flavors: Don't be afraid to try something new. The vendors in Santiago take great pride in their recipes, and each dish tells a story of tradition and innovation.
- Hygiene Matters: While street food can be incredibly delicious, it's important to choose vendors who maintain high standards of cleanliness. Look for vendors with a steady stream of customers, as this is often an indicator of quality and cleanliness.
- Cash is King: Many street food vendors may not accept cards, so it's a good idea to carry some cash. Additionally, smaller bills can be more convenient for transactions.

Sampling street food in Santiago is not just a culinary adventure, but also a cultural one. It's an opportunity to connect with the vibrant spirit of the city and taste the authentic flavors that define Dominican cuisine.

Dominican Coffee Tasting in Jarabacoa

Santiago, known as the "Heart City" of the Dominican Republic, boasts a vibrant street food scene that offers a delectable taste of local flavors and culinary traditions. Navigating the bustling streets of Santiago, you'll encounter a wide array of stalls and vendors, each with their own unique offerings. Here are some of the must-try street foods that define the culinary experience in this lively city.

Mangu con Los Tres Golpes

A quintessential Dominican breakfast, Mangu con Los Tres Golpes is a dish that exemplifies simplicity and bold flavors. It consists of mashed plantains, often seasoned with garlic and olive oil, served alongside three distinct accompaniments: fried cheese, salami, and eggs. The fusion of creamy mangu with the salty, savory elements creates a harmonious explosion of taste, making it a favorite among locals and visitors alike.

Chimis: Santiago's Savory Sandwiches

Chimis, a beloved Dominican fast food, are hearty sandwiches that reflect the cultural diversity of the island. These sandwiches feature a protein of your choice, often marinated and grilled to perfection, nestled within a soft, slightly crispy roll. Toppings range from crisp lettuce, tomatoes, and onions to zesty sauces, creating a symphony of flavors and textures. Whether you opt for the succulent pork, tender beef, or flavorful chicken, chimis are a must-try for any street food enthusiast in Santiago.

Yuca con Mojo

A staple side dish in Dominican cuisine, yuca con mojo is a simple yet incredibly satisfying treat. Yuca, a starchy root vegetable similar to cassava, is boiled until tender and served with a zesty garlic and citrus-based sauce known as mojo. The result is a dish that balances the earthy richness of the yuca with the bright, tangy notes of the sauce, creating a harmonious combination that captures the essence of Dominican comfort food.

Pastel en Hoja: A Tasty Wrapped Package

Pastel en hoja, a traditional Dominican dish, is a true culinary treasure. This dish involves seasoned meat (often pork or chicken) encased in a delicate layer of mashed green plantains, then wrapped in a banana leaf and steamed to perfection. The result is a succulent, flavorful package that exudes the essence of Dominican cuisine. The banana leaf imparts a subtle, earthy aroma to the dish, elevating the overall experience.

Tamarindo Candy and Other Sweet Delights
Santiago's street food scene isn't limited to savory offerings; it's also a haven for those with a sweet tooth. Tamarindo candy, made from the tangy pulp of the tamarind fruit, is a popular choice among locals. Its sweet and sour flavor profile provides a refreshing contrast to the rich and savory treats found throughout the city. Additionally, keep an eye out for dulces de coco (coconut candy) and crispy churros, both of which are bound to satisfy any sugary cravings.

Exploring the vibrant streets of Santiago and indulging in its diverse street food offerings is an essential part of experiencing the rich tapestry of Dominican culture. From savory classics like mangu and chimis to sweet treats like tamarindo candy, every bite tells a story of tradition, flavor, and the warm hospitality of the Dominican people. So, venture forth and savor the delightful treasures that await in Santiago's bustling food scene!

Chocolate Making Workshops in Puerto Plata

Puerto Plata, known for its stunning beaches and vibrant culture, also hides a sweet secret for chocolate lovers. Nestled amidst the lush cocoa plantations, you'll find an array of chocolate-making workshops that offer a unique and interactive experience for visitors.

Unraveling the Art of Chocolate Making
These workshops provide an immersive journey into the world of cacao, guiding participants through the entire

chocolate-making process. Led by skilled chocolatiers, you'll start by exploring the cacao groves, where you'll learn about the different varieties of cacao trees and how they are cultivated.

From Bean to Bar: A Hands-On Experience
Participants get their hands dirty (in the most delicious way possible!) as they assist in harvesting ripe cacao pods and extracting the beans. This tactile experience allows you to appreciate the craftsmanship involved in producing high-quality chocolate.

The next step involves fermenting and drying the beans, a crucial phase that greatly influences the flavor profile of the final product. Guided by experts, you'll learn the art of fermentation and drying techniques, gaining insight into the nuances that distinguish various chocolate varieties.

The Grind: Turning Beans into Cocoa Mass
One of the most fascinating aspects of the workshop is the grinding process. With traditional equipment, you'll grind the dried cacao beans into a smooth, aromatic cocoa mass. This step offers a sensory delight, as the rich scent of cocoa fills the air, immersing you in the heart of chocolate-making.

Infusion of Flavors: Adding Personal Touches
Once you have your cocoa mass, it's time to customize your chocolate. You'll experiment with different flavorings, from classic vanilla to exotic spices, creating a blend that suits your taste buds. This stage allows for creativity and personalization, making each participant's chocolate truly unique.

Molding and Tempering: Craftsmanship at Its Finest
After perfecting your chocolate blend, it's time to mold and temper it. With expert guidance, you'll pour your mixture

into molds, creating bars or unique shapes. Tempering, a crucial step in achieving a glossy finish and satisfying snap, requires precision and patience.

The Sweet Reward: Indulging in Your Creation

The moment arrives when you finally get to savor the fruits of your labor. You'll taste the chocolate you've crafted from scratch, savoring the complex flavors and aromas you helped bring to life. It's an incredibly gratifying experience, knowing that you played a vital role in creating this delectable treat.

Take Home a Taste of Puerto Plata

As a memento of your chocolate-making adventure, you'll be able to package your creations to bring home. This not only offers a tangible memory of your experience but also provides a delectable souvenir to share with friends and family.

Conclusion: A Sweet Memory to Treasure

Participating in a chocolate-making workshop in Puerto Plata is more than just a culinary adventure; it's an opportunity to connect with the rich cultural heritage of the region and gain a deeper appreciation for the art of chocolate-making. From the cacao groves to the final tasting, every step is a testament to the dedication and craftsmanship that goes into creating this beloved treat.

Chapter 6: Cultural Immersion

Attending a Merengue or Bachata Dance Workshop

One of the most authentic and vibrant ways to experience the heart of Dominican culture is through its music and dance. Merengue and Bachata, two of the country's most iconic musical genres, are deeply ingrained in the social fabric of the Dominican Republic. Attending a Merengue or Bachata dance workshop offers travelers a unique opportunity to connect with the rhythm and spirit of the nation.

The Rhythmic Heartbeat of Dominican Culture
Merengue, with its lively beat and infectious melodies, is often considered the national dance of the Dominican Republic. Its origins are deeply rooted in Afro-Caribbean and Spanish influences, making it a true reflection of the country's diverse heritage. In contrast, Bachata is a more soulful and romantic genre, originating in the rural areas of the Dominican Republic. Both dances have evolved over the years, incorporating modern elements while preserving their cultural essence.

Workshop Experience: Learning the Steps
Participating in a Merengue or Bachata dance workshop provides a hands-on experience in understanding the nuances of these dances. Knowledgeable instructors guide participants through the basic steps, teaching the proper posture, footwork, and hand movements that characterize each dance. The workshops are designed to cater to dancers of all levels, from beginners taking their first steps onto the dance floor to more experienced dancers looking to refine their technique.

Cultural Significance: Beyond the Dance Floor

Merengue and Bachata aren't merely dances; they're expressions of Dominican identity and emotions. Merengue, with its energetic tempo, is often associated with celebrations and joyous occasions. In contrast, Bachata's soulful melodies capture the depth of human emotions, telling stories of love, longing, and everyday life in the Dominican Republic. By learning these dances, travelers gain insight into the cultural narratives that have shaped the lives of the Dominican people for generations.

Connecting with Locals: Breaking Cultural Barriers

Attending a Merengue or Bachata dance workshop also provides a wonderful opportunity to interact with locals. Dance, being a universal language, transcends linguistic barriers and allows for meaningful connections with Dominican instructors and fellow participants. Through shared laughter and the universal language of movement, travelers often find themselves forging friendships that can last a lifetime.

Take Home a Piece of the Dominican Spirit

After attending a Merengue or Bachata dance workshop, participants often leave with more than just memories. They carry with them a newfound appreciation for the rich cultural tapestry of the Dominican Republic. Whether it's the spirited rhythms of Merengue or the heartfelt melodies of Bachata, these dances become a part of the traveler's own story, a tangible link to the vibrant soul of the Caribbean nation.

Attending a Merengue or Bachata dance workshop is an immersive cultural experience that leaves a lasting impression on travelers. It's an opportunity to not only learn the steps but to feel the heartbeat of Dominican culture.

Through dance, participants become part of a legacy that has been passed down through generations, connecting them with the people and traditions that define the spirit of the Dominican Republic.

Exploring the Larimar Mines in Barahona

Nestled in the rugged landscapes of Barahona, the Larimar mines offer a fascinating journey into the heart of a unique and mesmerizing gemstone. Known as the "Atlantis Stone" or the "Dolphin Stone," Larimar is a rare blue variety of the mineral pectolite, found exclusively in the Dominican Republic. The mines, situated in the southwest of the country, provide an opportunity for visitors to witness the extraction of this stunning gemstone and learn about its geological significance.

A Geological Marvel
Larimar's exquisite azure hue is the result of copper impurities within the pectolite structure. The stone's vibrant blue shades, ranging from pale sky blue to deeper oceanic tones, make it a highly sought-after gem among collectors and jewelry enthusiasts worldwide. The unique geological conditions that gave birth to Larimar are found in only a few locations on Earth, with the Dominican Republic being the primary source.

Guided Tours and Authentic Experiences
Visitors to the Larimar mines in Barahona are in for a memorable and educational experience. Guided tours are typically available, allowing guests to delve into the geological processes that created this extraordinary gem. Knowledgeable guides share insights into the formation of Larimar, explaining the intricate interplay of minerals and elements over millions of years.

The tours often take guests through the mining process, from the initial extraction to the careful cutting and polishing of the rough Larimar stones. This firsthand experience provides a deep appreciation for the craftsmanship involved in transforming raw minerals into the polished gems that adorn jewelry and art pieces.

Meeting Local Artisans
One of the most enriching aspects of exploring the Larimar mines is the opportunity to interact with local artisans and craftsmen. Many of these skilled individuals have honed their expertise over generations, passing down traditional techniques for working with Larimar. Visitors may have the privilege of observing these artisans at work, witnessing the meticulous skill and dedication that goes into crafting Larimar jewelry.

Ethical Mining Practices
The Larimar mines in Barahona are often committed to responsible and sustainable mining practices. This includes minimizing environmental impact and ensuring fair labor conditions for workers. By supporting these ethical operations, visitors can take pride in knowing that their interest in Larimar contributes to the well-being of both the local community and the natural environment.

Taking a Piece of Barahona Home
No visit to the Larimar mines is complete without the opportunity to acquire a piece of this exquisite gemstone. Visitors often have the chance to browse a selection of Larimar jewelry and art pieces, either directly from the mines or from nearby shops and galleries. Each piece carries with it a unique connection to the Dominican Republic's rich geological history.

Visiting a Dominican Cigar Factory

The Dominican Republic has earned a well-deserved reputation for producing some of the finest cigars in the world. A visit to a Dominican cigar factory offers a fascinating glimpse into the artistry and craftsmanship behind these sought-after tobacco products.

The Legacy of Dominican Cigars
The tradition of cigar-making in the Dominican Republic dates back centuries. The country's rich soil, combined with a favorable climate, provides the perfect conditions for cultivating high-quality tobacco leaves. This legacy, passed down through generations, is evident in the meticulous process employed in every cigar factory.

A Journey into Craftsmanship
Upon entering a Dominican cigar factory, visitors are immediately enveloped in the earthy aroma of tobacco leaves. Skilled artisans, often referred to as torcedores, work diligently at their stations, their nimble fingers expertly handling the leaves with precision and care. Each step of the process, from selecting the finest leaves to rolling and packaging, is a testament to the dedication and expertise of these craftsmen.

Leaf Selection and Sorting
The journey begins with the careful selection and sorting of tobacco leaves. The leaves are meticulously inspected for quality, texture, and color. Only the finest leaves, chosen for their rich flavors and smooth textures, make the cut. This initial step sets the foundation for the exceptional cigars that will be crafted.

Rolling Techniques
Watching the torcedores at work is a mesmerizing experience. With practiced hands, they skillfully roll the

selected leaves, ensuring a perfect blend of flavors and an even burn. The rolling process is an art form in itself, demanding both precision and finesse. It's a testament to the mastery that comes only with years of dedicated practice.

Aging and Fermentation
After the cigars are rolled, they undergo a crucial aging process. This stage allows the flavors to mature and develop, resulting in a smoother, more nuanced smoking experience. The cigars are carefully stored in cedar-lined rooms, where they rest for a period of time, absorbing the unique characteristics of the wood.

Quality Assurance
Quality control is paramount in a Dominican cigar factory. Every cigar undergoes rigorous inspections to ensure it meets the highest standards. From draw testing to the assessment of color and texture, each cigar is scrutinized to guarantee an exceptional smoking experience for the consumer.

The Culmination: Packaging and Presentation
Once the cigars have undergone the necessary aging and quality checks, they are meticulously packaged. The presentation of Dominican cigars is an art in itself, with attention to detail in every aspect, from the label design to the box construction. The final product is a testament to the pride and craftsmanship that goes into each and every cigar.

Artisan Craft Markets in Santo Domingo

Santo Domingo, the vibrant capital of the Dominican Republic, is not only steeped in history but also boasts a thriving artisan community. Nestled within its charming streets are a myriad of artisan craft markets, offering a treasure trove of handcrafted goods that reflect the rich cultural heritage of the island.

Exploring the Markets
Walking through the cobblestone alleys of Santo Domingo's craft markets is akin to embarking on a sensory journey. The markets are a riot of colors, with stalls brimming with intricate handwoven textiles, exquisitely carved wooden figurines, and dazzling jewelry adorned with locally sourced gemstones. Visitors can't help but be captivated by the sheer artistry and craftsmanship on display.

Taino Influence and Cultural Fusion
One can't delve into the world of Dominican artisan crafts without encountering the profound influence of the Taino people, the indigenous inhabitants of the island. Artisans often draw inspiration from Taino symbols and motifs, incorporating them into their creations. This infusion of indigenous heritage with elements from Spanish, African, and other cultures creates a unique and dynamic fusion in the crafts produced.

Textiles and Fabrics
One of the most enchanting aspects of Santo Domingo's craft markets is the array of textiles available. Skilled weavers employ age-old techniques, passed down through generations, to produce stunning fabrics. Vibrant tapestries, embroidered linens, and traditional garments known as "mangas" are just a few of the textile treasures awaiting visitors.

Woodwork and Carvings
Woodcarving is a revered art form in the Dominican Republic, and Santo Domingo's markets are veritable showcases for this craft. Master carvers transform native woods into exquisite sculptures and functional items. From

intricately detailed religious icons to whimsical animal figurines, each piece is a testament to the artisan's skill and passion.

Jewelry and Semiprecious Stones
The Dominican Republic is known for its abundance of semiprecious stones, including amber and larimar. Artisans skillfully incorporate these gems into their jewelry designs, resulting in pieces that are as unique as they are beautiful. Visitors to the markets will find an array of earrings, necklaces, and bracelets that showcase these stunning stones.

Supporting Local Artisans
Beyond the aesthetic appeal, purchasing crafts from Santo Domingo's markets is a meaningful way to support local artisans and their communities. Many of these artisans operate small, family-run businesses, and the income generated from their crafts plays a vital role in sustaining their way of life.

Preserving Cultural Heritage
By patronizing these markets, visitors actively contribute to the preservation of Dominican cultural heritage. The artisans are not only creators but also custodians of traditions that have endured for centuries. Their crafts serve as tangible links to the island's past, ensuring that these artistic legacies will continue to flourish for generations to come.

Traditional Festivals and Celebrations

The Dominican Republic is a vibrant tapestry of cultures, and this rich heritage is best showcased through its lively festivals and celebrations. Throughout the year, various towns and cities come alive with color, music, dance, and an infectious energy that invites both locals and visitors to join in the festivities.

Carnival in La Vega

One of the most exuberant celebrations in the Dominican Republic is the Carnival, and the city of La Vega hosts one of the most renowned Carnival festivities in the country. This event is a riot of creativity, with elaborate costumes, vibrant masks, and exquisitely choreographed dance routines. The air is filled with the infectious rhythms of merengue and bachata, and the streets become a pulsating sea of revelers. Carnival in La Vega is not only a celebration of Dominican culture but also a testament to the resilience and spirit of its people.

Semana Santa: Holy Week in Santo Domingo

Semana Santa, or Holy Week, is a significant religious celebration in the Dominican Republic. Santo Domingo, being the oldest European settlement in the Americas, holds a particularly poignant Semana Santa procession. Thousands of devout worshippers and curious onlookers gather to witness the reenactment of the Passion of Christ. Elaborate processions wind their way through the historic streets, with participants dressed in biblical attire, carrying symbols of the crucifixion.

Pueblo Nuevo Festival in Santiago

The Pueblo Nuevo Festival in Santiago is a testament to the Dominican Republic's African heritage. This lively celebration takes place in late May, paying homage to the country's Afro-Dominican roots. The streets come alive with vibrant costumes, African drumming, and pulsating rhythms. It's a time of cultural exchange, where traditional Afro-Dominican dances like the Palo and Guloyas are showcased alongside contemporary music styles.

Merengue Festival in Santo Domingo

As the birthplace of merengue, Santo Domingo hosts an annual Merengue Festival that draws music enthusiasts from all over the world. This event pays tribute to the infectious rhythms and lively dance moves that define this quintessential Dominican genre. The festival features performances by renowned merengue bands, as well as up-and-coming artists, creating an electric atmosphere that resonates with the heart and soul of the nation.

Fiesta de Palo in San Juan de la Maguana
The Fiesta de Palo is a unique celebration that originated in the San Juan province. It's a fusion of African, Spanish, and indigenous Taino influences, creating a distinctive cultural experience. The festival centers around traditional music, dance, and rituals associated with the Palo religion. This vibrant celebration showcases the resilience and cultural diversity that defines the Dominican Republic.

Chapter 7: Water Activities

Diving in Bayahibe's Coral Reefs

Bayahibe, a charming coastal village located on the southeastern coast of the Dominican Republic, is a haven for divers seeking to explore the mesmerizing underwater world of the Caribbean. The azure waters of the Bayahibe region boast some of the most diverse and vibrant coral reefs in the region, making it a premier destination for both novice and experienced divers alike.

The Underwater Landscape:
Submerged beneath the crystal-clear waters lie an array of coral formations, creating a kaleidoscope of colors and shapes. Bayahibe's coral reefs are a testament to the biodiversity of marine life in the Caribbean. Elkhorn coral, brain coral, and gorgonian sea fans stretch towards the surface, providing shelter and sustenance for an array of marine species.

Marine Fauna:
Diving in Bayahibe offers encounters with an astonishing variety of marine life. Schools of tropical fish, including vibrant parrotfish and striped sergeant majors, dart in and out of the corals. Eagle rays gracefully glide by, their wingspan captivating to behold. Lucky divers may even encounter a gentle nurse shark or a curious sea turtle, both of which are common inhabitants of these vibrant waters.

Dive Sites:
Bayahibe offers a range of dive sites to cater to divers of all levels of expertise. For beginners, the shallow, calm waters of sites like St. George Wreck provide a perfect introduction to the wonders of underwater exploration. This sunken cargo

ship, now an artificial reef, teems with marine life and offers a gentle descent into the world below.

Advanced divers, on the other hand, can venture to sites like Atlantic Princess Wreck. Resting at depths that challenge even the most seasoned divers, this sunken vessel is now an underwater playground for barracuda, moray eels, and other large predatory species.

Conservation Efforts:
Preserving the delicate ecosystem of Bayahibe's coral reefs is paramount. Local conservation initiatives and dive operators work tirelessly to promote responsible diving practices. Strict adherence to buoyancy control, avoiding contact with the corals, and refraining from collecting souvenirs helps to ensure that future generations can continue to enjoy this underwater wonderland.

Planning Your Dive:
When planning a diving excursion in Bayahibe, it's essential to choose a reputable dive operator. These professionals not only guide you through the breathtaking underwater landscapes but also prioritize safety and environmental conservation.

Remember to check your equipment, follow dive briefings diligently, and always dive within your certification limits. Underwater photography enthusiasts will find ample opportunities to capture the vibrant marine life, but remember to do so without disturbing the natural habitat.

Whale Watching in Samaná

Whale watching in Samaná is an awe-inspiring experience that allows visitors to witness one of the most majestic creatures on Earth - the humpback whale. Every year, from January to March, these magnificent creatures migrate from the icy waters of the North Atlantic to the warm and sheltered bay of Samaná to mate and give birth. This natural phenomenon has made Samaná one of the premier whale-watching destinations in the world.

The Migration Spectacle

The journey of the humpback whales to Samaná is a remarkable feat of nature. These gentle giants, known for their distinctive hump and long pectoral fins, travel thousands of miles to reach the Dominican coast. The warm and calm waters of Samaná Bay provide a sanctuary for them to carry out their crucial life processes. Witnessing these massive creatures breach, tail-slap, and blow spouts of water is an experience that leaves an indelible mark on any observer.

Guided Tours and Responsible Tourism

To ensure a safe and respectful encounter with these magnificent creatures, it's highly recommended to join a guided whale-watching tour. These tours are led by experienced local guides and certified naturalists who possess in-depth knowledge about the behavior and habitat of humpback whales. They are also well-versed in responsible whale-watching practices, which prioritize the well-being of the whales and their natural environment.

The Samaná Bay Sanctuary

Samaná Bay has been designated as a marine sanctuary, providing a protected environment for the humpback whales. This designation reflects the Dominican Republic's commitment to conservation and preserving its natural heritage. Strict regulations are in place to govern the activities of tour operators and to ensure that the whales are not disturbed or harmed in any way.

Tour Options and Packages
Visitors have a variety of tour options to choose from, ranging from half-day excursions to full-day immersive experiences. Some tours even offer opportunities for snorkeling or swimming in the vicinity of the whales, providing a truly unforgettable encounter with these gentle giants. Additionally, many tour operators offer educational components, providing participants with valuable insights into the biology and behavior of humpback whales.

Beyond Whale Watching
While the main attraction in Samaná is undoubtedly the humpback whales, the region offers a host of other activities and sights. Visitors can explore the lush El Limón rainforest, hike to the breathtaking El Limón waterfall, or relax on the pristine beaches that dot the coastline. The combination of whale watching and exploring the natural beauty of Samaná makes for a truly enriching and unforgettable experience.

Catamaran Tours in Punta Cana

Punta Cana, known for its pristine beaches and crystal-clear waters, offers a plethora of unforgettable experiences for travelers. One of the most enchanting adventures you can embark on is a Catamaran Tour. This excursion promises a day of relaxation, exploration, and aquatic wonder, all set against the backdrop of the Caribbean Sea.

Setting Sail
As you step aboard the luxurious catamaran, you'll immediately sense the spirit of adventure in the air. The crew, seasoned sailors with a deep love for the ocean, are eager to share their passion for Punta Cana's coastal beauty. The vessel, equipped with modern amenities and safety features, ensures a comfortable journey for all passengers.

Cruising the Caribbean

The catamaran gently glides over the turquoise waters, offering panoramic views of Punta Cana's coastline. The gentle sea breeze caresses your skin, and the rhythmic lull of the waves creates a soothing ambiance. You'll have ample opportunities to bask in the sun on spacious decks or unwind in shaded lounging areas.

Snorkeling Extravaganza

One of the highlights of a Catamaran Tour is the chance to explore the vibrant underwater world of Punta Cana. The catamaran anchors at carefully selected snorkeling spots, where the crew provides top-notch snorkeling gear and expert guidance. As you dip beneath the surface, you'll find yourself surrounded by a kaleidoscope of marine life: colorful corals, exotic fish, and perhaps even curious sea turtles.

Hidden Coves and Pristine Beaches

The catamaran tour unveils hidden coves and secluded beaches, accessible only by sea. These pristine sanctuaries offer a stark contrast to the bustling resorts of Punta Cana. You'll have the opportunity to disembark and set foot on soft, powdery sands, where the clear waters lap at the shore invitingly.

Culinary Delights and Refreshments

A Catamaran Tour is not only a visual feast but a culinary one as well. The onboard chefs prepare delectable local and international dishes, using fresh, seasonal ingredients. From succulent seafood to tropical fruits, every bite is a celebration of Caribbean flavors. Complementing the cuisine is an array of refreshing beverages, including exotic cocktails and chilled, local beverages.

Music, Dance, and Caribbean Vibes

As the sun begins its descent, the catamaran comes alive with the beats of Caribbean music. The crew members, known for their infectious energy and love for dance, encourage guests to join in the festivities. Whether you're swaying to the rhythm or trying your hand at merengue, the experience is bound to leave you with cherished memories.

Sunset Spectacle

As evening approaches, the catamaran sets course for a prime vantage point to witness the breathtaking Caribbean sunset. The sky transforms into a canvas of fiery oranges, purples, and pinks, casting a spellbinding glow over the horizon. It's a moment of pure magic that captures the essence of Punta Cana's natural beauty.

Conclusion: A Day to Remember

A Catamaran Tour in Punta Cana is more than a maritime adventure; it's a journey into the heart of the Caribbean's splendor. With its blend of relaxation, exploration, and cultural immersion, this experience is bound to be a highlight of your Dominican Republic getaway.

Fishing Excursions in Cabo Rojo

Nestled on the southwestern coast of the Dominican Republic, Cabo Rojo is a hidden gem for fishing enthusiasts seeking a serene and bountiful angling experience. With its pristine waters, abundant marine life, and breathtaking coastal scenery, this quaint fishing village offers an idyllic setting for both novice and seasoned anglers.

The Abundance of Marine Life

Cabo Rojo is renowned for its rich biodiversity, making it a haven for various fish species. The warm Caribbean waters teem with an array of marine life, including snapper, grouper, mahi-mahi, and even the elusive marlin. The diverse underwater ecosystem provides a fertile ground for a successful fishing expedition.

Types of Fishing Excursions
Visitors to Cabo Rojo can choose from a variety of fishing excursions tailored to their preferences and skill levels.

1. Deep-Sea Fishing:

For the adventurous angler, deep-sea fishing charters venture into the open waters of the Caribbean Sea. Here, you'll have the chance to reel in trophy-sized game fish, such as tuna and billfish. The experienced local guides, familiar with the region's top fishing spots, ensure a thrilling and fruitful adventure.

2. Inshore Fishing:

If you prefer calmer waters and a more relaxed pace, inshore fishing in the nearby bays and mangroves is an excellent choice. This option is ideal for families or those looking to enjoy a leisurely day on the water. Expect to encounter species like snook, tarpon, and redfish.

3. Fly Fishing:

Cabo Rojo's shallow flats and mangrove-lined estuaries provide a perfect habitat for fly fishing. This method allows for a more immersive and challenging experience, as you'll need to cast your line with precision to entice the local bonefish, permit, and snook.

The Local Fishing Culture
One of the unique aspects of fishing in Cabo Rojo is the opportunity to engage with the local fishing community. The village has a deeply ingrained fishing culture, and many of

the guides are seasoned fishermen who have honed their skills over generations. They're not only experts in the craft of fishing but also knowledgeable about the marine ecology and the best practices for sustainable angling.

Planning Your Fishing Excursion
Before embarking on a fishing excursion in Cabo Rojo, it's recommended to book a reputable charter or guide service in advance. They can provide valuable insights on the best times to fish, depending on your target species, as well as any necessary permits or licenses.

Additionally, it's essential to pack appropriate sun protection, comfortable clothing, and any personal fishing gear you may prefer. Most charters provide the necessary equipment, but avid anglers may have specific preferences.

Surfing in Encuentro Beach

Located on the north coast of the Dominican Republic, Encuentro Beach has earned a reputation as one of the premier surfing destinations in the Caribbean. This picturesque stretch of coastline, just a short drive from the lively town of Cabarete, offers consistent waves and a laid-back atmosphere that beckons surfers of all skill levels.

The Waves:
Encuentro Beach is renowned for its consistent and varied waves, making it an ideal spot for both beginners and experienced surfers. The beach features a reef break that produces left and right-handers, providing ample opportunities for riders to catch a wave that suits their preference. The waves here range from gentle rollers for novices to more challenging barrels for the seasoned surfers, ensuring there's something for everyone.

Surf Schools and Lessons:
For those new to the sport or looking to refine their skills, Encuentro Beach boasts a thriving surf school scene. Experienced instructors are on hand to offer lessons tailored to individual needs. They focus on everything from paddling techniques to reading waves and maintaining proper form. With patient guidance, beginners can find their footing, while intermediate and advanced surfers can fine-tune their abilities.

Surfing Community:
Encuentro Beach has cultivated a vibrant and welcoming surfing community. Surfers from all around the world come together here, creating an inclusive atmosphere that encourages camaraderie and shared stoke. Whether you're catching waves for the first time or a seasoned pro, you're likely to find like-minded individuals to share the surf with.

Equipment Rental and Shops:
For those who haven't brought their own gear, Encuentro Beach offers a range of surfboard rentals. From soft-top beginner boards to high-performance shortboards, there's a selection to suit all skill levels and wave conditions. Additionally, there are surf shops nearby where you can purchase or rent other essentials like wetsuits, leashes, and wax.

Beyond Surfing:
While Encuentro Beach is primarily known for its waves, there's more to explore in the surrounding area. Nearby, you'll find charming cafes and beachside restaurants where you can refuel after a session in the water. Additionally, the lush green hills and scenic viewpoints offer a picturesque backdrop for those looking to take a break from the surf.

Tips for Surfers:
Check the Surf Forecast: Before heading out, it's advisable to check the surf forecast. Websites and apps dedicated to surfing often provide up-to-date information on wave height, direction, and wind conditions.

Respect Local Rules: Familiarize yourself with any local surfing etiquette or rules. This includes respecting right of way and adhering to any posted guidelines.

Safety First: Always prioritize safety. Be aware of your abilities and the conditions, and consider wearing appropriate safety gear like a leash.

Surfing in Encuentro Beach offers an unforgettable experience for surf enthusiasts of all levels. Whether you're a beginner looking to catch your first wave or an experienced surfer seeking a new challenge, the waves here promise an exhilarating ride in the heart of the Dominican Republic.

Chapter 8: Relaxation and Wellness

Spa Retreats in Punta Cana

Punta Cana, known for its pristine beaches and luxurious resorts, also offers a haven for relaxation and rejuvenation in the form of world-class spa retreats. Nestled amidst the lush tropical landscape and overlooking the azure Caribbean Sea, these spas provide a sanctuary for travelers seeking solace and wellness.

Serene Environments and Holistic Treatments
Punta Cana's spa retreats are renowned for their serene environments, often set in idyllic locations with breathtaking views. Upon arrival, guests are enveloped in an atmosphere of tranquility, where the sound of gently lapping waves and the scent of tropical blooms create an immediate sense of calm.

The treatments offered are deeply rooted in holistic practices, drawing inspiration from local traditions and global wellness techniques. Skilled therapists, trained in various massage modalities and holistic therapies, customize each session to address individual needs. From traditional Swedish massages to indigenous treatments utilizing local ingredients like coconut oil and aloe vera, every experience is tailored to provide the highest level of relaxation and rejuvenation.

Signature Experiences and Wellness Programs
Many of the spa retreats in Punta Cana boast a curated menu of signature experiences. These exclusive treatments are designed to offer a unique and unforgettable spa journey. Guests can indulge in rituals inspired by the natural

elements, such as volcanic stone massages or oceanic seaweed wraps, allowing them to connect with the essence of the Caribbean.

Additionally, wellness programs are available for those seeking a more comprehensive approach to health and vitality. These programs often include a combination of spa treatments, fitness activities, and nutritional guidance. Guests can embark on a holistic wellness journey, leaving them feeling not only relaxed but also revitalized and balanced.

Eco-Friendly and Sustainable Practices
Many of the spa retreats in Punta Cana are committed to eco-friendly and sustainable practices. They often utilize organic, locally sourced ingredients in their treatments and incorporate green initiatives into their daily operations. Some even offer eco-conscious spa products for guests to continue their wellness routines at home.

Furthermore, some spa retreats participate in community outreach and conservation efforts, contributing to the preservation of the region's natural beauty. This commitment to sustainability enhances the overall experience, allowing guests to not only relax but also feel good about their contribution to the environment.

Beyond the Spa: Wellness Amenities
In addition to their world-class spa facilities, many retreats in Punta Cana offer a range of wellness amenities. These may include yoga and meditation pavilions, fitness centers, and healthy dining options. Guests are encouraged to embrace a holistic approach to their well-being, allowing them to nurture their body, mind, and spirit throughout their stay.

Yoga and Meditation in Las Galeras

Nestled on the northeastern coast of the Dominican Republic, Las Galeras offers a serene sanctuary for travelers seeking solace, self-discovery, and rejuvenation through yoga and meditation. This picturesque village, surrounded by lush greenery and pristine beaches, provides an idyllic setting for practitioners of all levels.

The Yoga Retreats of Las Galeras
Las Galeras boasts a vibrant yoga community, with various retreat centers and studios scattered across the landscape. These retreats often combine the natural beauty of the area with purpose-built facilities designed for yoga and meditation practices. Many of them offer daily classes, workshops, and immersive retreats led by experienced instructors.

Finding Inner Balance in Nature's Embrace
One of the most compelling aspects of practicing yoga and meditation in Las Galeras is the connection to nature. Imagine performing your sun salutations with the sound of waves crashing in the background or meditating amidst the rustling palm fronds. The tranquil surroundings create a harmonious environment that enhances the mind-body connection, allowing for a deeper spiritual experience.

Diverse Styles and Approaches
Whether you're a seasoned yogi or a novice looking to embark on your spiritual journey, Las Galeras caters to a wide range of preferences and skill levels. From the meditative flow of Hatha to the dynamic movements of Vinyasa, and the grounding postures of Ashtanga, you'll find a variety of styles to explore. Additionally, some retreats offer specialized classes such as Kundalini or Restorative

yoga, allowing practitioners to delve into specific aspects of their practice.

Guidance from Expert Instructors

The yoga instructors in Las Galeras are renowned for their expertise, compassion, and dedication to guiding students on their path to self-discovery. Many have extensive training in various yoga disciplines, meditation techniques, and holistic wellness practices. They create a nurturing space for participants to explore their practice, offering personalized adjustments and mindful guidance.

Beyond Asana: Meditation and Mindfulness

While yoga postures (asanas) are a fundamental aspect of the practice, Las Galeras also provides a rich environment for those seeking to deepen their meditation practice. Whether it's guided meditation sessions, mindfulness workshops, or silent retreats, you'll have ample opportunities to cultivate a sense of inner stillness and presence.

Community and Camaraderie

Participating in yoga and meditation in Las Galeras not only nurtures your individual practice but also allows you to connect with like-minded individuals from around the world. Many retreats offer communal dining areas and shared accommodations, fostering a sense of community and camaraderie among participants.

Practical Considerations

Before embarking on your yoga and meditation journey in Las Galeras, it's advisable to check the offerings and schedules of the various retreat centers. Some may require advance booking, while others offer drop-in classes. Additionally, consider bringing comfortable yoga attire, a mat, and an open heart ready for self-discovery.

In Las Galeras, the union of yoga, meditation, and the natural world creates a transformative experience for practitioners. Whether you're seeking physical flexibility, mental clarity, or a deeper spiritual connection, this coastal haven provides the perfect backdrop for your journey within. Embrace the opportunity to harmonize with the rhythms of nature and your own inner rhythms in this enchanting corner of the Dominican Republic.

Hot Springs in La Ciénaga

La Ciénaga, a small town nestled in the southwestern region of the Dominican Republic, is home to a hidden gem that offers visitors a unique and rejuvenating experience: natural hot springs. Tucked away amidst lush tropical vegetation, these thermal pools have long been cherished by locals for their purported therapeutic properties and are now gaining popularity among travelers seeking relaxation and healing in a serene natural setting.

The Natural Wonders of La Ciénaga
The hot springs in La Ciénaga owe their existence to the geological activity that characterizes this region. Underground volcanic chambers heat the water, enriching it with minerals known for their soothing and healing effects on the body. As the water emerges to the surface, it forms a series of pools nestled within a tranquil forested area.

The Healing Properties
Many believe that the mineral-rich waters of La Ciénaga's hot springs hold a myriad of health benefits. The high mineral content, including sulfur, calcium, and magnesium, is said to alleviate muscle pain, improve circulation, and promote relaxation. Additionally, the warm temperature of the springs encourages the release of endorphins, providing a natural mood boost. Visitors often find relief from

conditions like arthritis, joint pain, and skin disorders after immersing themselves in these therapeutic waters.

A Tranquil Retreat
The setting of La Ciénaga's hot springs adds to the overall experience. Surrounded by dense foliage, the pools are shaded by towering trees that create a canopy, allowing dappled sunlight to filter through. The gentle rustling of leaves and the distant calls of tropical birds contribute to the serene ambiance, making it an idyllic spot for relaxation and contemplation.

A Cultural Experience
Beyond their natural allure, the hot springs in La Ciénaga are deeply woven into the local culture. Families from nearby towns have been visiting these springs for generations, passing down traditional practices and stories associated with the healing waters. Visitors have the opportunity to engage with the friendly locals, gaining insight into the rich cultural heritage that surrounds this natural oasis.

Practical Information
For those planning a visit, it's advisable to arrive early in the day to avoid crowds. There are basic facilities available, including changing rooms and restroom facilities. Visitors are encouraged to bring their own towels and refreshments, as the area maintains its natural, uncommercialized charm.

Conservation Efforts
Preserving the natural environment surrounding the hot springs is a priority for both locals and conservationists. Efforts are underway to implement sustainable practices, ensuring that future generations can continue to enjoy this therapeutic sanctuary.

Natural Mud Baths in Barahona

Nestled along the southwestern coast of the Dominican Republic lies the coastal gem of Barahona, a region known for its stunning natural beauty and unique geological features. One of the most intriguing and rejuvenating experiences that Barahona offers is its natural mud baths.

The Healing Powers of Mud

The mud baths of Barahona are situated in a tranquil enclave surrounded by lush greenery and the soothing sounds of nature. What makes this experience truly special is the therapeutic properties of the mud found in the region. Rich in minerals, volcanic ash, and organic matter, the mud is believed to have healing and rejuvenating effects on the skin.

The Process

Visitors are welcomed to the mud baths by knowledgeable guides who explain the history and benefits of this natural spa treatment. The mud is carefully harvested from specific areas, ensuring its purity and effectiveness.

Guests are then invited to apply the mud to their skin, creating a unique and refreshing mask that covers the body. The texture is smooth, cool, and luxuriously silky, making the application a delight in itself. As the mud dries, it begins to tighten on the skin, creating a gentle exfoliating effect that removes impurities and dead skin cells.

Relaxation in Nature's Embrace

As the mud works its magic, visitors are encouraged to relax and soak in the serene surroundings. The natural setting enhances the therapeutic experience, with the scent of wildflowers in the air and the distant sound of birdsong. It's a moment of pure connection with nature, a pause from the fast pace of everyday life.

Rinsing in the Caribbean Waters
After the mud has dried and worked its wonders, guests are guided to the nearby azure waters of the Caribbean Sea. Here, they wash off the mud, revealing incredibly soft, rejuvenated skin beneath. The contrast of the warm sun, cool sea, and refreshed skin is invigorating and truly revitalizing.

A Sense of Renewal
Many who experience the natural mud baths of Barahona speak of a profound sense of renewal and well-being. The minerals and elements in the mud are believed to promote circulation, soothe aches and pains, and leave the skin feeling soft and supple. It's not just a physical transformation, but a deeply refreshing and invigorating experience for both body and mind.

Sustainability and Respect for Nature
Guides emphasize the importance of preserving the natural environment in which the mud baths are located. Sustainable practices are employed to ensure that future generations can also enjoy this unique experience.

Beachfront Massages in Juan Dolio

Nestled along the shimmering coastline of the Dominican Republic, Juan Dolio offers a tranquil escape for travelers seeking both relaxation and rejuvenation. One of the most blissful experiences this coastal gem has to offer is the exquisite beachfront massages. Here, the rhythmic sound of the waves and the gentle caress of the sea breeze create a perfect backdrop for a therapeutic escape.

The Serenity of Beachfront Massages
As you settle onto the soft, warm sands, the skilled hands of experienced masseuses gently begin to work their magic. The

natural elements of Juan Dolio add an extra layer of serenity to the experience. The soothing symphony of the waves harmonizes with the gentle strokes, creating a transcendent atmosphere that lulls you into a state of complete relaxation.

Traditional Techniques, Modern Comfort
The massage therapists in Juan Dolio are trained in a variety of techniques, ranging from Swedish and deep tissue to hot stone therapy. They skillfully blend traditional methods with modern practices, ensuring that each session is tailored to your specific needs. Whether you seek to release tension in your muscles or simply wish to indulge in pure relaxation, these therapists have the expertise to deliver a truly transcendent experience.

Aromatherapy and Healing Oils
The use of high-quality aromatherapy oils is a hallmark of the beachfront massages in Juan Dolio. These oils are carefully selected for their therapeutic properties, enhancing the overall experience. The fragrant essences envelop you in a cocoon of calm, heightening the benefits of the massage and leaving you with a sense of renewed vitality.

The Benefits Beyond Relaxation
Beyond the immediate sense of tranquility, beachfront massages in Juan Dolio offer a range of health benefits. The improved blood circulation helps to alleviate muscle tension, reduce stress levels, and enhance overall well-being. Moreover, the soothing environment and skilled techniques contribute to mental clarity and a profound sense of inner peace.

Unparalleled Oceanfront Views
What sets the beachfront massages in Juan Dolio apart is the stunning backdrop of the Caribbean Sea. As you sink into a state of bliss, your senses are treated to the sight of azure

waters stretching endlessly towards the horizon. The rhythmic ebb and flow of the waves create a mesmerizing visual symphony that complements the soothing touch of the massage.

Tailored Packages for Every Preference
Whether you prefer a solo session, a couples' massage, or even a group experience, Juan Dolio offers a range of packages to suit every preference. Additionally, many establishments provide additional amenities such as private cabanas, refreshing beverages, and post-massage relaxation areas, allowing you to extend the experience and savor the tranquility.

A Timeless Retreat
The beachfront massages in Juan Dolio are more than a luxury; they are a timeless retreat that invites you to connect with the natural beauty of the Dominican Republic. In this coastal paradise, the union of skilled therapy, soothing surroundings, and the healing power of the sea creates an experience that transcends the ordinary, leaving you with a sense of profound serenity and renewal.

Chapter 9: Nightlife and Entertainment

Salsa Dancing in Santo Domingo

Santo Domingo, the vibrant capital city of the Dominican Republic, pulsates with the rhythm of salsa. This lively dance form, born from a blend of Afro-Caribbean and Latin influences, finds its heart and soul in the colorful streets and lively nightclubs of Santo Domingo.

The Salsa Scene
Santo Domingo boasts a thriving salsa scene that caters to dancers of all levels. Whether you're a seasoned pro or just starting out, there's a place for you to immerse yourself in the infectious beats and energetic moves of salsa.

Dance Clubs and Hotspots
El Sartenazo:

Located in the heart of the Colonial Zone, El Sartenazo is a popular haunt for salsa enthusiasts. The intimate setting and live bands create an electrifying atmosphere that keeps dancers moving till the early hours.

Gozando en la Habana:

This lively venue is known for its authentic Cuban atmosphere. With skilled instructors offering dance lessons early in the evening, Gozando en la Habana caters to both novices and seasoned dancers.

MamaJuana Cafe:

Situated in the upscale Piantini neighborhood, MamaJuana Cafe seamlessly blends contemporary style with a vibrant

Latin ambiance. The dance floor comes alive after sunset, inviting patrons to showcase their salsa skills.

Onnos Bar:

Onnos Bar is a beloved spot for locals and tourists alike. Its diverse music selection spans from classic salsa to the latest reggaeton hits. The friendly atmosphere encourages dancers to let loose and enjoy the night.

Salsa Lessons
For those looking to refine their moves or take their first steps onto the dance floor, Santo Domingo offers a plethora of dance schools and instructors. Many establishments provide group classes, private lessons, and workshops tailored to different skill levels.

Special Events and Salsa Festivals
Santo Domingo hosts numerous salsa events and festivals throughout the year. These gatherings bring together dancers from all over the world to celebrate the joy of salsa. The annual Santo Domingo Salsa Festival, for instance, is a highlight for many, featuring world-class performances, workshops, and electrifying dance parties.

Embracing the Culture
Beyond the dance floor, salsa in Santo Domingo is a cultural experience. It's an opportunity to connect with locals, learn about the rich history of the dance, and immerse oneself in the vibrant energy that defines this dynamic city.

Safety and Considerations
While Santo Domingo is generally a safe city, it's always advisable to take standard precautions when venturing out at night. Stick to well-populated areas, keep an eye on your

belongings, and consider traveling in groups, especially if you're unfamiliar with the area.

Beach Parties in Punta Cana

Punta Cana, known for its stunning beaches and vibrant nightlife, is the ultimate destination for beach parties that pulse with energy and excitement. As the sun dips below the horizon, the coastline transforms into a dynamic playground of music, dance, and celebration.

The Rhythmic Heartbeat of Punta Cana Nights
When night falls in Punta Cana, the atmosphere comes alive with the beat of Dominican music, blending the infectious rhythms of Merengue, Bachata, and Reggaeton. The beachfront venues, adorned with colorful lights and swaying palm trees, create a magical backdrop for unforgettable gatherings.

Iconic Venues
Among the renowned venues for beach parties is the legendary Coco Bongo. Located right on the beach, this world-famous club is a sprawling entertainment complex that seamlessly combines music, dance, and theatrical performances. Here, guests can revel in a high-energy atmosphere that fuses the excitement of a beach party with the allure of a Las Vegas-style show.

For those seeking a more intimate experience, Soles Chill Out Bar is a hidden gem. Nestled on the shores of Bavaro Beach, it offers a laid-back yet electrifying ambiance. Guests can sink their feet into the warm sands while sipping exotic cocktails and grooving to the latest beats.

Themed Extravaganzas
Beach parties in Punta Cana often feature themed extravaganzas that add an extra layer of excitement. From

glow parties with neon body paint to Caribbean Carnival-inspired celebrations, each event promises a unique and immersive experience. Fire dancers, acrobats, and DJs adept at reading the crowd all contribute to the vibrant tapestry of entertainment.

Sunset Soirees
One of the most enchanting aspects of beach parties in Punta Cana is the opportunity to witness breathtaking sunsets over the Caribbean Sea. As the sky paints itself in warm hues, partygoers gather on the sand, creating a sense of camaraderie that transcends language and borders. This magical moment sets the stage for an unforgettable night of revelry.

Culinary Delights and Libations
Apart from the pulsating beats, beach parties in Punta Cana also boast an array of delectable culinary offerings. Freshly grilled seafood, tropical fruits, and local specialties tantalize the taste buds. The cocktail menus are equally impressive, featuring an array of signature concoctions that perfectly complement the lively atmosphere.

A Fusion of Cultures
Punta Cana's beach parties draw an international crowd, creating a melting pot of cultures and languages. This diversity adds a dynamic dimension to the festivities, fostering an inclusive environment where everyone can share in the joy of the moment.

Jazz and Blues in Cabarete
Cabarete, known for its vibrant beach culture and water sports, also harbors a hidden gem for music enthusiasts – a thriving jazz and blues scene that adds a soulful touch to this coastal paradise.

The Musical Ambiance

As the sun sets and the rhythmic crashing of waves provides a natural backdrop, Cabarete transforms into a haven for lovers of jazz and blues. The warm Caribbean breeze carries the mellowness of the music through the air, creating an enchanting atmosphere.

Venues and Performances

Several venues in Cabarete showcase talented musicians, both local and international, who come together to create unforgettable performances. Among them, the "Jazz & Blues Lounge" stands out as a hub for live music. Nestled along the beach, this intimate venue regularly hosts bands and solo artists, offering an eclectic mix of jazz standards, bluesy ballads, and even some Caribbean-infused renditions.

Local and International Talent

One of the remarkable aspects of Cabarete's jazz and blues scene is its diverse lineup of performers. While local Dominican artists bring their unique flavor to the stage, international musicians also frequent the scene, enriching the musical tapestry. This fusion of styles and influences creates an experience that resonates with audiences from all walks of life.

Musical Events and Festivals

Beyond the regular performances, Cabarete hosts various jazz and blues festivals throughout the year. These events draw in a wide array of talent and music enthusiasts, turning the town into a lively celebration of sound. The Cabarete Jazz Festival, in particular, stands as a testament to the town's commitment to nurturing its musical culture.

Intimate Encounters with Artists

One of the distinct charms of Cabarete's jazz and blues scene is the accessibility to the artists themselves. After a performance, it's not uncommon for musicians to mingle with the audience, sharing stories and insights into their craft. This personal connection enhances the overall experience, leaving visitors with a deeper appreciation for the music and the artists who bring it to life.

A Fusion of Cultures
The jazz and blues scene in Cabarete mirrors the rich tapestry of cultures that define the Dominican Republic. It's a melting pot of influences, where African rhythms intertwine with European melodies, and Caribbean flair adds a distinctive touch. This fusion of cultures is not only heard in the music but felt in the very spirit of the performances.

Casino Nights in Santo Domingo

Santo Domingo, the vibrant capital of the Dominican Republic, is not only known for its rich history and lively culture but also for its thriving nightlife. One of the city's prime attractions for those seeking an exciting evening out is its array of world-class casinos.

The Glittering Scene:
As the sun sets over the Caribbean horizon, Santo Domingo transforms into a city that never sleeps. The casinos here are more than just places to try your luck; they are glamorous entertainment hubs that offer a taste of high-stakes excitement amidst a backdrop of opulence and luxury. From the moment you step through their doors, you're greeted by the soft glow of chandeliers, the hum of lively conversations, and the unmistakable energy of a place where fortunes can change in an instant.

Gaming Choices:
Santo Domingo's casinos cater to a diverse range of preferences. Whether you're a seasoned gambler or a casual player looking for a night of entertainment, there's

something for everyone. The gaming floors boast an extensive selection of options, from classic table games like blackjack, roulette, and poker to an impressive array of modern slot machines, all impeccably maintained and overseen by professional dealers and attendants.

Exquisite Amenities:
Beyond the gaming action, the casinos in Santo Domingo offer a wealth of amenities to ensure your experience is nothing short of exceptional. Lavish bars serve up expertly crafted cocktails, fine wines, and premium spirits, providing the perfect setting to toast to your successes or savor the moment regardless of the outcome on the tables. Gourmet restaurants within the establishments present a diverse menu of culinary delights, ranging from international cuisine to local delicacies prepared by top-tier chefs.

Entertainment Extravaganza:
The entertainment extends far beyond the casino floors. Many venues feature live performances, including concerts by world-renowned artists, electrifying dance shows, and themed events that add an extra layer of excitement to your night out. The pulsating beats of Latin music may draw you onto the dance floor, where you can join locals and fellow travelers in a rhythmic celebration of life.

Responsible Gaming:
While the allure of the casino can be irresistible, it's important to approach the experience with a sense of responsibility. Santo Domingo's casinos prioritize responsible gaming, offering resources and assistance for those who may need it. Staff members are trained to identify signs of compulsive gambling and are always available to provide guidance or support if necessary.

Planning Your Casino Night:

Before heading out for a night of gaming and entertainment, it's advisable to check the dress code and any entrance requirements of the specific casino you plan to visit. Some venues may have certain policies in place to maintain an upscale atmosphere. Additionally, be sure to set a budget for your evening to ensure that your casino night remains a fun and enjoyable experience.

In Santo Domingo, the thrill of a casino night is elevated by the city's unique blend of Caribbean warmth and cosmopolitan sophistication. Whether you're testing your luck at the tables or simply soaking in the electrifying ambiance, a night in one of Santo Domingo's renowned casinos promises memories that will last a lifetime.

Live Music in Puerto Plata

This coastal city has a rich musical heritage, blending indigenous rhythms with African, European, and Caribbean influences, creating a unique and infectious sound that permeates the streets and venues of Puerto Plata.

The Rhythmic Heartbeat of Puerto Plata
Music is an integral part of Dominican culture, and Puerto Plata exemplifies this with its plethora of live music venues. From traditional merengue and bachata to reggaeton and salsa, the city offers a diverse range of genres to cater to all musical tastes.

Historic Venues and Modern Beats
One of the most iconic venues for live music in Puerto Plata is the historic Amber Museum. Nestled within an 18th-century Victorian mansion, this venue not only showcases the beauty of amber but also hosts regular musical performances. Imagine listening to the soulful melodies of local artists amidst the backdrop of vintage architecture - it's an experience that transcends time.

For those seeking a more contemporary vibe, the Malecón De Puerto Plata is the place to be. This seaside promenade comes alive at night with the beats of local bands and international DJs. You can sway to the rhythm of the waves while enjoying a cocktail and immersing yourself in the pulsating energy of the crowd.

Traditional Tunes and Dancefloor Delights
No visit to Puerto Plata would be complete without experiencing the enchanting sounds of traditional Dominican music. Many venues offer live performances of merengue and bachata, where local musicians expertly play the accordion, tambora, and güira, creating a lively atmosphere that is sure to get you on your feet.

If you're in the mood for something a bit more upbeat, salsa clubs like "La Costanera" and "Rumba Cafe" offer the perfect setting. Skilled dancers glide across the floor as live bands set the tempo, creating an electrifying atmosphere that invites everyone to join in the celebration.

Intimate Performances and Big Concerts
While Puerto Plata is known for its lively nightlife, it also offers more intimate settings for music enthusiasts. Cozy cafes and small taverns often host acoustic sessions, allowing you to enjoy the raw talent of local musicians up close and personal. It's a chance to savor the nuances of their craft and perhaps even strike up a conversation with the artists themselves.

For those seeking larger-scale concerts, Puerto Plata occasionally hosts international acts and music festivals. These events draw crowds from near and far, creating an electric atmosphere that showcases the city's ability to host world-class entertainment.

A Melodic Finale to Your Puerto Plata Adventure

As the night winds down, you'll find that the music in Puerto Plata is more than just entertainment; it's a cultural experience that leaves a lasting impression. Whether you're dancing under the stars or swaying to the rhythms in an intimate venue, the live music scene in Puerto Plata is a testament to the city's vibrant soul and the indomitable spirit of its people. Don't miss the opportunity to immerse yourself in this musical tapestry during your visit to Puerto Plata.

Chapter 10: Wildlife Encounters

Visiting the Jaragua National Park

Located in the southwestern region of the Dominican Republic, Jaragua National Park is a pristine natural sanctuary that offers a diverse range of ecosystems and wildlife. Covering an area of approximately 1,850 square kilometers, it is the largest national park in the Caribbean.

The park is renowned for its striking coastal landscapes, featuring dramatic cliffs that overlook the azure waters of the Caribbean Sea. These cliffs provide nesting grounds for numerous seabird species, including the endangered Ridgway's Hawk.

In addition to its coastal splendor, Jaragua National Park is home to a variety of terrestrial and marine habitats. Visitors have the opportunity to explore dry forests, mangrove swamps, and pristine beaches. The park also encompasses a marine reserve, protecting extensive coral reefs and underwater biodiversity.

One of the highlights of a visit to Jaragua National Park is the chance to observe the native wildlife. The park is home to a rich array of species, including the endangered American Crocodile, West Indian Manatee, and a diverse range of bird species such as flamingos, herons, and pelicans.

Exploring the park can be done through a network of well-marked trails, allowing visitors to immerse themselves in the natural beauty and observe the wildlife in its natural habitat. There are also opportunities for snorkeling and diving to discover the vibrant marine life beneath the surface.

Preservation efforts have been implemented to protect the delicate ecosystems within the park, making it an important site for conservation and research. As a visitor, you'll have the chance to appreciate the significance of this ecological gem and contribute to its ongoing protection.

Overall, a visit to Jaragua National Park promises a captivating blend of natural beauty, biodiversity, and conservation efforts. Whether you're a nature enthusiast, birdwatcher, or simply seeking a serene escape, this national park offers a truly immersive experience in the heart of the Dominican Republic's natural wonders.

Birdwatching in Los Haitises

Los Haitises National Park, nestled along the northeastern coast of the Dominican Republic, is a haven for bird enthusiasts. This protected area boasts a rich diversity of avian species, making it a prime destination for birdwatching.

The park's lush mangroves, limestone formations, and pristine wetlands provide an ideal habitat for a wide array of birdlife. Here, you can witness both migratory and resident species in their natural environment.

As you venture into this ecological treasure trove, keep an eye out for the striking plumage of the Hispaniolan parrot, an endemic species that calls this park home. Listen for the distinctive calls of the mangrove cuckoo and the melodious song of the black-whiskered vireo, which are often heard echoing through the mangrove forests.

Additionally, the park is frequented by several species of herons, egrets, and ibises. The great blue heron, with its impressive stature, is a common sight, gracefully wading through the shallow waters in search of prey. Keep your binoculars at the ready to catch a glimpse of the reddish egret, known for its vibrant plumage and unique hunting behavior.

For the avid birder, Los Haitises offers an opportunity to spot migratory birds, especially during the winter months. Species like the osprey and the peregrine falcon are known to visit, providing a thrilling sight for those lucky enough to witness their aerial displays.

In addition to its avian treasures, Los Haitises offers a captivating landscape, with its dramatic limestone karsts and emerald-green waters. This makes for an immersive birdwatching experience, where you can appreciate both the natural beauty of the surroundings and the diverse birdlife that inhabits them.

Remember to bring your binoculars, a field guide, and a keen sense of observation to make the most of your birdwatching adventure in Los Haitises National Park. Whether you're a seasoned birder or a novice enthusiast, this unique ecosystem is sure to leave you with cherished memories and a newfound appreciation for the avian wonders of the Dominican Republic.

Exploring the Cotubanamá National Park

Nestled on the southern coast of the Dominican Republic, Cotubanamá National Park offers a captivating blend of biodiversity and historical significance. Stretching across lush tropical forests and pristine coastline, this protected area provides a haven for both nature enthusiasts and history buffs.

Flora and Fauna

The park boasts an astonishing array of flora and fauna, showcasing the rich biodiversity of the region. Towering mahogany trees and ancient guanacaste canopies dominate the landscape, providing shelter to an array of wildlife. Birdwatchers will delight in the chance to spot colorful species like the Hispaniolan parrot and the palmchat, while lucky visitors may even catch a glimpse of the elusive solenodon, one of the world's rarest mammals.

The Taino Legacy

Cotubanamá National Park holds great cultural significance, as it was once inhabited by the indigenous Taino people. Traces of their presence can still be found in the form of petroglyphs and cave art, offering a fascinating glimpse into their ancient way of life. Exploring these historical remnants provides a profound connection to the island's heritage.

Cueva del Puente

One of the park's highlights is the Cueva del Puente, a mesmerizing limestone cave that conceals an underground river. The cave's unique geological formations and shimmering subterranean pools create an otherworldly atmosphere, inviting adventurous souls to delve deeper into the heart of the earth.

Coastal Wonders

Beyond the lush interior, Cotubanamá National Park also offers a spectacular coastline, where rugged cliffs meet the crystal-clear Caribbean Sea. The dramatic juxtaposition of land and water creates an awe-inspiring backdrop for beachcombing and coastal exploration. Be sure to keep an eye out for marine life; dolphins and sea turtles are known to frequent these waters.

Trails and Hiking

For those seeking a more active adventure, the park features a network of well-marked trails that wind through its diverse landscapes. From leisurely strolls to more challenging hikes, visitors can choose their own path to explore the park's natural wonders. Each trail unveils a different facet of the park, from dense forests to hidden waterfalls.

Practical Tips

- Guided Tours: Consider joining a guided tour led by knowledgeable local experts. They can provide invaluable insights into the park's ecology and history.
- Pack Essentials: Don't forget to bring essentials like water, sunscreen, insect repellent, and comfortable footwear for hiking.
- Respect Wildlife and Heritage: Help preserve the park's natural and cultural treasures by refraining from disturbing wildlife or tampering with historical artifacts.
- Leave No Trace: Practice responsible tourism by leaving the park as you found it, without litter or damage.

Exploring Cotubanamá National Park is a journey into the heart of the Dominican Republic's natural and cultural heritage, where every step reveals a new layer of its remarkable beauty. Whether you're drawn to its diverse ecosystems or its rich historical tapestry, this park offers an unforgettable adventure for all who visit.

Dolphin Encounters in Punta Cana

Dolphin encounters in Punta Cana offer a unique opportunity to get up close and personal with these intelligent and playful marine creatures. The warm, crystal-clear waters of the Caribbean provide an ideal setting for this unforgettable experience.

At carefully selected marine parks, you'll have the chance to interact with dolphins in their natural habitat while trained professionals ensure both your safety and the well-being of the dolphins. These encounters often include educational sessions about dolphin behavior, habitat, and conservation efforts.

Punta Cana's dolphin encounters typically allow guests to swim, play, and even receive a friendly dorsal fin ride from these gentle giants. Additionally, some programs offer the chance to participate in hands-on training sessions, providing a deeper understanding of dolphin behavior and communication.

It's important to choose a reputable operator that adheres to ethical and sustainable practices. By participating in a responsible dolphin encounter, you not only create lasting memories but also support conservation efforts aimed at protecting these magnificent creatures and their habitats. Remember to bring your waterproof camera to capture these magical moments!

Turtle Watching in Bahia de las Aguilas

The pristine shores of Bahia de las Aguilas offer a unique opportunity to witness one of nature's most fascinating spectacles: the nesting of sea turtles. This secluded beach, located within the protected Jaragua National Park, serves as a sanctuary for several species of sea turtles, including the critically endangered Hawksbill and Leatherback turtles.

During the nesting season, which typically spans from April to July, visitors have the chance to observe these ancient creatures as they make their way ashore to lay their eggs. Guided tours, led by knowledgeable naturalists, provide a respectful and educational experience, ensuring minimal disturbance to the nesting process.

Under the soft glow of the moon, the beach becomes a sanctuary of natural wonder. As the waves gently lap against the shore, the turtles laboriously dig their nests, depositing clutches of eggs before carefully covering them with sand. Witnessing this awe-inspiring ritual is a poignant reminder of the importance of conservation efforts to protect these magnificent creatures and their fragile habitats.

It's crucial to remember that while this experience is undoubtedly captivating, it's essential to follow all guidelines provided by park rangers and tour guides to ensure the safety and well-being of both visitors and turtles alike. This includes maintaining a respectful distance, refraining from flash photography, and avoiding any disruptive behavior.

Turtle watching in Bahia de las Aguilas is not only a chance to witness a natural wonder but also an opportunity to become a steward for the conservation of these remarkable marine creatures. By treading lightly and respecting their space, visitors can play a crucial role in ensuring the continued survival of sea turtles for generations to come.

Chapter 11: Hidden Gems and Off-the-Beaten-Path Adventures

Exploring the Remote Playa Rincón

Nestled along the northeastern coast of the Samaná Peninsula, Playa Rincón stands as a testament to untouched natural beauty. This remote gem remains one of the Dominican Republic's best-kept secrets, captivating intrepid travelers with its pristine shores and lush, verdant surroundings.

A Journey Off the Beaten Path
To reach Playa Rincón, one must embark on a journey that feels like stepping back in time. The road leading to this secluded haven is rugged, winding through dense tropical forests and small villages, offering glimpses into the daily lives of the locals. Along the way, the landscape transforms, revealing stunning vistas of the turquoise Atlantic Ocean, creating a sense of anticipation and adventure.

The Allure of Playa Rincón
Upon arrival, Playa Rincón reveals itself in all its unspoiled glory. Stretching for over three kilometers, the beach boasts powdery, golden sands that invite visitors to kick off their shoes and feel the warmth beneath their feet. The backdrop is equally captivating, with towering coconut palms swaying in the gentle sea breeze and vibrant vegetation providing a lush contrast against the azure waters.

Tranquil Bliss and Secluded Solitude

One of the defining characteristics of Playa Rincón is its peaceful atmosphere. Unlike some of the more bustling beaches in the Dominican Republic, this remote paradise offers a sense of seclusion that is truly unparalleled. Visitors often find themselves sharing the expanse of shoreline with only a handful of like-minded explorers, allowing for an intimate connection with nature and a genuine escape from the pressures of everyday life.

Aquatic Adventures
The calm, crystal-clear waters of Playa Rincón are ideal for a variety of water activities. Snorkeling enthusiasts will delight in the vibrant marine life that flourishes along the coral reefs just offshore. Schools of colorful fish dart in and out of the coral formations, creating an underwater spectacle that rivals even the most renowned diving spots in the Caribbean.

Picnics and Beachside Delights
For those seeking a peaceful retreat, Playa Rincón offers a picture-perfect setting for a beachside picnic. Many visitors choose to pack a hamper with local delicacies, such as ripe plantains, fresh coconuts, and succulent seafood, creating a delightful culinary experience against the backdrop of the sea.

Sunset Serenity
As the day gently fades into evening, Playa Rincón transforms yet again. The setting sun casts a warm, golden glow across the landscape, painting the sky with hues of pink and orange. It's a moment of pure serenity, a time to reflect on the beauty of the natural world and the privilege of experiencing such a remote and untouched paradise.

A Memory to Treasure
Exploring Playa Rincón is more than a beach day; it's an immersive journey into nature's purest form. Whether you're

seeking solitude, adventure, or simply a respite from the ordinary, this hidden gem in the Dominican Republic offers an experience that lingers in the memory long after the journey home.

Hiking to the El Limón Waterfall

Nestled within the lush greenery of the Samaná Peninsula, the El Limón Waterfall stands as a testament to the raw natural beauty that the Dominican Republic has to offer. This majestic cascade, plummeting from a height of over 50 meters, is a true gem for nature enthusiasts and adventure seekers alike. The journey to reach this stunning sight is an adventure in itself, taking you through dense forests, across rustic bridges, and immersing you in the vibrant biodiversity of the region.

The Trailhead
The hike to El Limón begins at the small village of El Limón, which is approximately a 30-minute drive from the town of Samaná. Here, visitors have the option to hire local guides who are well-versed in the terrain and can offer valuable insights into the flora and fauna of the region. The trailhead is marked by a rustic sign, and from here, the adventure truly begins.

A Journey Through Nature's Bounty
The trail winds its way through thickets of tropical vegetation, with vibrant orchids and towering ferns creating a lush canopy overhead. The air is filled with the sweet scent of wildflowers, and the sounds of birdsong echo through the forest. As you progress along the path, you'll encounter small streams and rivulets, their waters crystal clear and inviting, offering a refreshing respite from the tropical heat.

Crossing Bridges and Forging Streams

One of the highlights of this trek are the charming wooden bridges that span the streams along the way. These rustic structures, crafted by local artisans, add a touch of enchantment to the journey. Crossing them, you'll catch glimpses of colorful fish darting through the clear waters below.

The Final Ascent
As you approach the waterfall, the trail becomes steeper, providing a thrilling sense of anticipation. The sound of rushing water grows louder, heightening the excitement. Emerging from the dense foliage, you'll be greeted by a breathtaking sight – El Limón, a powerful cascade, cascading down the rugged cliff face and into a crystal-clear pool below.

Taking in the Splendor
Arriving at the base of the waterfall, visitors are treated to a mesmerizing display of natural beauty. The pool at the foot of El Limón invites weary hikers to take a refreshing dip, providing a perfect opportunity to cool off after the invigorating hike. The brave-hearted can even approach the falls for a natural massage courtesy of the cascading water.

Conservation and Sustainability
Preserving the natural habitat around El Limón Waterfall is of paramount importance. Local communities and environmental organizations work together to maintain the integrity of this ecological treasure. Visitors are encouraged to adhere to Leave No Trace principles, ensuring that this pristine environment remains unspoiled for generations to come.

In the heart of the Dominican Republic, the El Limón Waterfall beckons adventurers to discover its beauty. The journey to this natural wonder is a testament to the wonders of the country's biodiversity and the warm hospitality of its people. For those seeking an authentic encounter with nature, this hike is an absolute must.

Discovering the Magic of Bahoruco

Nestled in the southwestern region of the Dominican Republic, the Bahoruco province is a hidden gem waiting to be explored. This enchanting area boasts a rich tapestry of natural wonders, cultural heritage, and adventures that will leave any traveler in awe.

Exploring the Bahoruco National Park
One of the crown jewels of this province is the Bahoruco National Park, a UNESCO-designated biosphere reserve. Spanning over 1,200 square kilometers, this park is a sanctuary for biodiversity, housing a stunning array of flora and fauna. Towering mahogany trees, vibrant orchids, and elusive wildlife like the Hispaniolan parrot find refuge within this lush expanse.

For nature enthusiasts and avid hikers, the park offers a network of well-maintained trails that wind through diverse ecosystems. One can embark on journeys that lead to panoramic viewpoints, hidden waterfalls, and serene lagoons. The park's rugged terrain presents a captivating challenge for seasoned trekkers, while also providing opportunities for leisurely strolls through its more accessible areas.

The Enigmatic Petroglyphs of Cueva de las Maravillas
A testament to the rich history of the Taino people, Bahoruco is also home to the Cueva de las Maravillas (Cave of Wonders). This archaeological site is adorned with ancient petroglyphs, offering a captivating glimpse into the beliefs and artistry of the indigenous inhabitants. Guided tours unravel the stories behind these enigmatic carvings,

providing a deeper appreciation for the cultural heritage of the Dominican Republic.

Charm of Barahona, the Provincial Capital
The provincial capital, Barahona, is a vibrant town nestled between the azure waters of the Caribbean Sea and the dramatic landscapes of the Bahoruco mountain range. Visitors can meander through its colorful streets, experiencing the warm hospitality of the locals and savoring the flavors of authentic Dominican cuisine in family-owned eateries.

Barahona is also a gateway to some of the most spectacular beaches in the region. Playa San Rafael's golden sands and crystalline waters offer a tranquil escape, while Playa Quemaito's rugged coastline provides a dramatic backdrop for sunsets that are nothing short of breathtaking.

A Haven for Birdwatchers
Bahoruco's diverse ecosystems make it a haven for birdwatchers and ornithologists. The area is home to an impressive array of avian species, including the endangered Hispaniolan parakeet and the striking Hispaniolan trogon. Birdwatching tours led by knowledgeable guides offer enthusiasts the chance to spot these feathered wonders in their natural habitats.

Cultural Encounters in Remote Villages
Venturing further into Bahoruco, travelers have the opportunity to engage with the local communities in remote villages. These encounters provide a window into the traditional way of life, where time seems to stand still. From artisanal crafts to folkloric music and dance, these villages offer a genuine immersion into Dominican culture.

In Bahoruco, nature's grandeur and human history converge in a mesmerizing display of beauty and heritage. This province invites intrepid travelers to uncover its secrets, promising an unforgettable journey through a land where magic is woven into every landscape and cultural encounter.

Laguna El Dudú: A Natural Wonder

Nestled within the lush landscapes of the Dominican Republic lies a hidden gem, Laguna El Dudú. This enchanting oasis, located near the town of Cabrera, is a true testament to the country's natural beauty and biodiversity. With its crystal-clear waters and surrounding verdant forests, Laguna El Dudú offers a serene retreat for both nature enthusiasts and adventure seekers alike.

The Magic of El Dudú
Upon arriving at Laguna El Dudú, visitors are greeted by a sight that seems almost surreal. The lake's pristine waters shimmer with a brilliant turquoise hue, inviting all who come to take a refreshing dip. Surrounded by dense foliage, the area exudes a sense of tranquility that immediately transports visitors away from the hustle and bustle of urban life.

The Twin Lagoons
What sets Laguna El Dudú apart is its unique geological formation, characterized by two interconnected lagoons, aptly named Laguna El Dudú Grande and Laguna El Dudú Chico. The larger of the two, El Dudú Grande, is a sprawling expanse of water, while El Dudú Chico is more secluded and nestled amidst the trees. Both lagoons offer distinct experiences, allowing visitors to choose between a lively atmosphere or a more secluded, intimate setting.

Exploring the Surroundings
For those seeking adventure, Laguna El Dudú offers a range of activities to satisfy every inclination. Adventurous souls

can explore the rugged terrain surrounding the lagoons through a network of well-maintained hiking trails. These trails lead to breathtaking viewpoints, revealing panoramic vistas of the lagoons and the surrounding landscape.

Water Adventures
The real magic of Laguna El Dudú, however, lies in its waters. Visitors can take advantage of various water-based activities, including kayaking, paddleboarding, and even cliff jumping for the thrill-seekers. The lake's crystal-clear depths provide a window into an underwater world teeming with aquatic life, making it a popular spot for snorkeling enthusiasts.

Flora and Fauna
Beyond the water's edge, the surrounding forest is a haven for biodiversity. Towering trees with sprawling canopies provide shelter for a wide array of bird species, making it a paradise for birdwatchers. Vibrant orchids and other tropical flora adorn the landscape, creating a rich tapestry of color and life.

Responsible Tourism
Preserving the natural beauty of Laguna El Dudú is of paramount importance. Visitors are encouraged to follow sustainable tourism practices, including disposing of waste responsibly and refraining from disturbing the local wildlife. By respecting this fragile ecosystem, we can ensure that future generations can also enjoy the wonders of Laguna El Dudú.

Remote Villages and Cultural Experiences

While the Dominican Republic is known for its vibrant cities and popular tourist destinations, venturing into its remote villages unveils a side of the country steeped in authentic culture and tradition. These tucked-away communities offer a glimpse into the heart of Dominican life, providing enriching experiences for travelers seeking genuine connections and a deeper understanding of local customs.

Connecting with Locals

One of the most rewarding aspects of visiting remote villages is the opportunity to connect with the locals. Warm smiles and open hearts welcome visitors, making them feel like part of the community. Conversations flow effortlessly, and stories are shared, bridging any cultural gaps and fostering a sense of camaraderie.

Traditional Crafts and Artisan Workshops

Remote villages often preserve age-old crafting techniques that have been passed down through generations. Visitors can witness skilled artisans creating intricate pieces of pottery, woven textiles, and handmade jewelry. These crafts offer insight into the rich artistic heritage of the Dominican Republic, and travelers may even have the chance to try their hand at these time-honored skills.

Culinary Experiences

Sampling local cuisine is an essential part of any cultural journey, and remote villages offer a unique twist on Dominican dishes. Visitors can savor traditional recipes prepared with locally-sourced ingredients, often harvested from the village's own gardens. From hearty stews to freshly baked bread, every meal tells a story of heritage and sustenance.

Participating in Festivals and Celebrations

Remote villages are the guardians of many traditional Dominican festivals and celebrations. These vibrant events are steeped in history and religious significance, providing a window into the spiritual and cultural practices of the community. Joining in the festivities, whether it's a lively carnival or a solemn religious procession, offers an unforgettable glimpse into the heart of Dominican culture.

Eco-Tourism Initiatives
Many remote villages are nestled in pristine natural surroundings, making them ideal hubs for eco-tourism initiatives. Guided nature walks, birdwatching tours, and even sustainable agriculture experiences are common offerings. These activities not only showcase the incredible biodiversity of the Dominican Republic but also contribute to the conservation efforts of the local community.

Preserving Cultural Heritage
Visiting remote villages contributes to the preservation of Dominican cultural heritage. By engaging with the local economy and supporting artisan crafts, visitors play a crucial role in sustaining these traditions for future generations. Additionally, the exchange of stories and experiences fosters a mutual respect for different ways of life.

In essence, exploring remote villages in the Dominican Republic is an enriching and transformative experience. It allows travelers to step off the beaten path and immerse themselves in the authentic rhythm of Dominican life. From connecting with welcoming locals to participating in age-old traditions, each moment in these villages is a treasure trove of cultural discovery. So, set forth and let the hidden gems of the Dominican countryside captivate your heart and soul.

Chapter 12: Adventure Sports and Extreme Activities

Paragliding Over Jarabacoa Valley

Paragliding over Jarabacoa Valley is an experience that promises an adrenaline rush like no other. Nestled in the heart of the Dominican Republic, Jarabacoa is renowned for its stunning natural beauty, with lush mountains, cascading waterfalls, and the winding Yaque del Norte River. This picturesque setting provides an ideal backdrop for an unforgettable paragliding adventure.

As you stand on the launch site, a sense of excitement and anticipation fills the air. The instructors, seasoned professionals with years of experience, ensure that you are equipped with the necessary safety gear and provide a thorough briefing on paragliding techniques. They also take the time to address any concerns or questions you may have, putting your mind at ease before takeoff.

Once harnessed securely to your experienced tandem pilot, you're ready for the thrill of a lifetime. With a few brisk steps, you'll find yourself effortlessly lifted off the ground, soaring into the azure sky. The initial rush of wind against your face is exhilarating, and as you ascend higher, the sweeping views of Jarabacoa Valley unfold below.

From your vantage point high above, you'll have an unparalleled perspective of the valley's natural wonders. The emerald canopy of tropical forests stretches as far as the eye can see, interrupted only by the occasional ribbon of a sparkling stream. The distant peaks of the Central Mountain

Range create a dramatic panorama, and if you're lucky, you might even catch a glimpse of colorful parrots or other exotic bird species in flight.

The sensation of flying is remarkably serene. Unlike other extreme sports, paragliding offers a sense of weightlessness and freedom that is both peaceful and awe-inspiring. You'll have the opportunity to communicate with your pilot, exchanging observations and soaking in the shared wonder of this unique experience.

As you glide through the thermals, you might catch sight of fellow paragliders in the distance, each carving their own graceful path through the sky. It's a communal dance with nature, a symphony of flight set against a backdrop of unparalleled natural beauty.

The descent, controlled by your expert pilot, is just as smooth and controlled as the ascent. With gentle turns and swoops, you'll gradually make your way back to solid ground. As you touch down, a wave of exhilaration and accomplishment washes over you.

Reflecting on your paragliding adventure over Jarabacoa Valley, you'll carry with you not only the memory of the breathtaking scenery but also a profound sense of connection with the natural world. It's an experience that lingers long after the adrenaline subsides, a testament to the wonders that await those willing to take the leap and soar.

In the end, paragliding over Jarabacoa Valley is not just an adventure; it's a transformative journey that leaves you with a renewed appreciation for the beauty and majesty of the Dominican Republic. It's an experience that beckons you to return, to once again take flight and explore the boundless skies above this tropical paradise.

Deep-Sea Diving in Bayahibe

Bayahibe, nestled along the southeastern coast of the Dominican Republic, is a haven for avid divers and underwater enthusiasts. Renowned for its crystal-clear waters, vibrant marine life, and a diverse range of dive sites, this coastal paradise offers an unparalleled deep-sea diving experience.

The Underwater Wonderland
Diving in Bayahibe is like entering a mesmerizing world beneath the waves. The vibrant coral reefs, ancient shipwrecks, and an array of marine species make this region a prime destination for divers of all levels. The pristine waters of the Caribbean Sea provide excellent visibility, often exceeding 30 meters, ensuring that every dive is a visual feast.

The Diverse Marine Life
One of the main draws of diving in Bayahibe is the opportunity to encounter a rich tapestry of marine life. Schools of tropical fish in kaleidoscopic hues dart around the corals, while graceful sea turtles glide through the water, seemingly undisturbed by the presence of divers. Moray eels peek out from crevices, and colorful sea anemones sway with the currents. Lucky divers might even catch a glimpse of the elusive seahorse or a well-camouflaged octopus.

Dive Sites for Every Skill Level
Bayahibe offers an extensive range of dive sites, catering to divers with varying levels of experience. Novices can explore the shallow, calm reefs where the water is teeming with life. Advanced divers can venture to deeper sites, where fascinating geological formations and more elusive species await discovery.

For those seeking an adrenaline rush, the "St. George" shipwreck is a must-visit. This sunken cargo ship, resting on the ocean floor, has become an artificial reef and a thriving ecosystem for marine creatures. Exploring its nooks and crannies is like stepping into a time capsule of maritime history.

The Dive Centers and Expert Guides
Bayahibe boasts a plethora of reputable dive centers staffed by certified instructors and experienced guides. These professionals are intimately familiar with the local underwater terrain and can tailor dives to suit the preferences and experience levels of each diver. Safety is paramount, and all equipment is meticulously maintained, ensuring a secure and enjoyable diving experience.

Conservation Efforts and Responsible Diving
The diving community in Bayahibe is deeply committed to preserving the delicate marine ecosystem. Many dive centers actively participate in conservation initiatives, including reef restoration projects and regular underwater clean-up efforts. Divers are encouraged to adhere to responsible diving practices, such as buoyancy control and not disturbing the marine life.

Beyond the Dive
While the underwater world is undeniably the main attraction, Bayahibe offers a wealth of activities for divers and non-divers alike. The charming village exudes a laid-back Caribbean vibe, with colorful houses, local eateries, and inviting beaches. Nearby excursions to the Saona Island and the Cotubanamá National Park provide opportunities for above-water adventures, including snorkeling in idyllic lagoons and exploring pristine forests.

ATV Off-Roading Adventures

One of the most exhilarating ways to do so is through ATV (All-Terrain Vehicle) off-roading adventures. This chapter is dedicated to the heart-pounding experiences and breathtaking sights that await those who embark on this adrenaline-fueled journey.

Exploring the Wild Terrain
ATV off-roading in the Dominican Republic offers an up-close encounter with nature's raw beauty. Guided by seasoned experts, adventurers traverse through dense forests, winding trails, and untamed countryside. The trails wind through lush tropical forests, riverbeds, and rugged mountainsides, providing an intimate connection with the island's natural splendor.

Diverse Routes for All Levels
Whether you're a seasoned off-road enthusiast or a first-timer, there are routes tailored to different skill levels. Beginners can enjoy more leisurely rides along well-maintained trails, while advanced riders can tackle challenging terrains, including steep inclines, rocky descents, and creek crossings. The variety ensures that everyone can partake in this high-octane adventure.

Scenic Vistas and Hidden Gems
Along the way, participants are treated to awe-inspiring vistas that are otherwise inaccessible. From panoramic views of the Caribbean Sea to hidden waterfalls and remote villages, ATV off-roading unveils the Dominican Republic's lesser-known treasures. Capturing these moments on camera is a must, as they serve as lasting memories of a truly unique adventure.

Environmental Stewardship

Guided ATV tours in the Dominican Republic prioritize eco-friendly practices and responsible tourism. Tour operators are committed to preserving the natural habitats and ecosystems that make these excursions possible. This includes adhering to designated trails, minimizing soil erosion, and respecting wildlife habitats. By choosing a reputable tour operator, participants can be assured that their adventure is conducted in harmony with the environment.

Safety First
Safety is paramount in ATV off-roading adventures. Participants are provided with safety gear, including helmets, gloves, and protective eyewear. Experienced guides offer thorough briefings on ATV operation, ensuring that riders feel confident and secure throughout the journey. Additionally, all vehicles undergo regular maintenance and safety checks to guarantee a smooth and secure ride.

Creating Lasting Memories
ATV off-roading adventures in the Dominican Republic offer a unique blend of excitement, exploration, and natural beauty. Whether it's a solo adventure or a group outing, the memories forged on these rugged trails are bound to be cherished for years to come. The camaraderie among fellow adventurers and the sense of accomplishment from conquering challenging terrains create an experience that lingers long after the journey ends.

Kitesurfing on the North Coast
The North Coast of the Dominican Republic is renowned for its stunning beaches, vibrant culture, and rich marine life. But for adventure seekers and water sports enthusiasts, it offers something even more exhilarating: world-class kitesurfing opportunities.

The Ideal Conditions

With its consistent trade winds and warm waters, the North Coast provides an ideal setting for kitesurfing. The steady breeze creates perfect conditions for both beginners and experienced kitesurfers alike. Cabarete, in particular, has gained international recognition as one of the premier kitesurfing destinations in the world.

Cabarete: Kitesurfing Paradise

Nestled along the coast, Cabarete boasts a unique blend of natural beauty and a thriving water sports community. Its crescent-shaped bay, fringed by swaying palm trees, provides an idyllic backdrop for kitesurfing enthusiasts. The shallow, crystal-clear waters near the shore are perfect for learning the basics, while the waves farther out offer a challenge for advanced riders.

Lessons for All Levels

Cabarete is home to numerous kitesurfing schools staffed by certified instructors. Whether you're a complete beginner or looking to refine your skills, you'll find tailored lessons to suit your level of experience. Safety is a top priority, and instructors provide thorough briefings on equipment, wind patterns, and safety protocols.

The Thrill of Riding the Wind

Once you've mastered the basics, the real fun begins. Feeling the power of the wind propelling you across the water is a sensation like no other. With the right technique, you'll be gliding, jumping, and even performing tricks in no time. The North Coast's varied conditions provide ample opportunities to progress and challenge yourself.

Connecting with Nature

Kitesurfing isn't just about the adrenaline rush; it's also about immersing yourself in nature. As you ride the waves, you'll have the chance to observe marine life below the surface. Keep an eye out for colorful fish darting among the coral formations, and if you're lucky, you might even spot a sea turtle or a playful dolphin.

A Thriving Community
Cabarete's kitesurfing community is a close-knit group of enthusiasts from around the world. Whether you're a solo traveler or part of a group, you'll find camaraderie among fellow kitesurfers. The beachfront bars and cafes are perfect for swapping stories and tips, creating a vibrant social scene that complements the thrill of the sport.

Beyond Kitesurfing
While kitesurfing takes center stage, the North Coast offers a host of other activities to complement your adventure. Explore the lush hinterlands on horseback, take a relaxing yoga class on the beach, or venture into nearby towns to experience the local culture and cuisine.

Canyoning in the El Limón Canyon

Nestled in the heart of the Dominican Republic, the El Limón Canyon offers an exhilarating canyoning experience like no other. This natural wonder, characterized by its steep rock walls, lush vegetation, and cascading waterfalls, provides an ideal playground for adrenaline seekers and nature enthusiasts alike.

The Adventure Begins
The adventure kicks off with a scenic hike through dense tropical forests. Guided by seasoned experts well-versed in the terrain, you'll meander along rugged trails, crossing wooden bridges and streams, as the anticipation builds for what lies ahead.

As you approach the mouth of the canyon, the air becomes charged with excitement. The sound of rushing water serves as a prelude to the breathtaking sights that await you. The sheer magnitude of the canyon's walls, cloaked in vibrant greenery, is awe-inspiring.

Gear Up for the Descent

Before venturing further, guides will provide a comprehensive safety briefing and outfit you with top-notch canyoning equipment. Harnesses, helmets, and specialized rappelling gear are meticulously checked to ensure a secure and thrilling experience.

Descending the Waterfalls

The true essence of canyoning lies in the descent of waterfalls, and the El Limón Canyon offers a series of them, ranging from moderate to adrenaline-pumping. Each descent is a unique challenge, and the guides are there to provide expert advice and assistance, making it accessible to both beginners and experienced canyoneers.

The adrenaline rush as you step off the ledge and begin your controlled descent is unmatched. The cool mist of the waterfall kisses your skin, and the roar of cascading water envelops your senses. The feeling of conquering nature's obstacles is nothing short of empowering.

Immersed in Natural Beauty

Between descents, take a moment to soak in the pristine beauty that surrounds you. The walls of the canyon seem to touch the sky, adorned with ferns and other lush vegetation clinging to the rocks. The calls of tropical birds echo through the gorge, creating a symphony that harmonizes with the rush of water.

A Test of Skill and Endurance

Canyoning in the El Limón Canyon is not just an adrenaline rush; it's a test of skill, endurance, and mental fortitude. Navigating the terrain requires a blend of agility, balance, and strategic thinking. Each step, each rappel, is a triumph over the forces of nature.

Chapter 13: Tips for Travelers

Packing Essentials

Packing for a trip to the Dominican Republic requires careful consideration of the tropical climate and the diverse range of activities you'll be engaging in. Here are some essential items to ensure a comfortable and enjoyable stay:

1. Lightweight and Breathable Clothing:
The Dominican Republic boasts warm weather throughout the year, so packing lightweight, breathable clothing is crucial. Opt for cotton or linen fabrics that allow air circulation and help keep you cool. Don't forget to include comfortable walking shoes for exploring beaches, hiking trails, and historic sites.

2. Sun Protection:
The Caribbean sun can be intense, so come prepared with sun protection essentials. Pack a wide-brimmed hat, sunglasses with UV protection, and a high-SPF sunscreen. Consider a reef-safe sunscreen if you plan on swimming in ecologically sensitive areas.

3. Swimwear:
Given the abundance of pristine beaches and water activities, having a few sets of swimwear is essential. Whether you're lounging on the sand or snorkeling in crystal-clear waters, comfortable and functional swimwear is a must.

4. Insect Repellent:
While the Dominican Republic isn't particularly plagued by mosquitoes, especially in well-populated areas, it's still a good idea to pack insect repellent. For eco-adventures or

visits to more remote regions, it becomes especially important.

5. Travel Adapters and Chargers:
The Dominican Republic typically uses Type A and B outlets, so ensure you have the appropriate travel adapters for your electronic devices. Don't forget chargers for your phone, camera, and other gadgets to capture all the memorable moments.

6. Reusable Water Bottle:
Staying hydrated in the Caribbean heat is crucial. Pack a reusable water bottle to refill throughout the day. It's both eco-friendly and cost-effective, and it ensures you always have access to clean drinking water.

7. First Aid Kit:
While you can find pharmacies in most towns, having a basic first aid kit is a wise precaution. Include items like bandages, antiseptic cream, pain relievers, and any personal medications you may need.

8. Light Rain Gear:
The Dominican Republic experiences occasional rain showers, especially during the rainy season. Pack a compact, lightweight rain jacket or a foldable umbrella to stay dry during unexpected downpours.

9. Travel Documents and Identification:
Ensure you have all necessary travel documents, including your passport, visa (if required), flight tickets, accommodation reservations, and any travel insurance documents. It's also a good idea to have photocopies or digital copies stored securely.

10. Daypack or Beach Bag:

A small daypack or a sturdy beach bag is invaluable for carrying essentials like water, sunscreen, snacks, and a towel when you're out and about exploring or relaxing on the beach.

11. Language Guide or Translator App:
While English is widely spoken in tourist areas, having a basic understanding of Spanish can greatly enhance your experience. Consider bringing a pocket-sized language guide or downloading a translation app for easy communication.

By packing these essentials, you'll be well-prepared for an unforgettable adventure in the Dominican Republic, ensuring a comfortable and enjoyable trip. Remember to also leave some space in your luggage for any unique souvenirs you might find along the way!

Safety and Health Considerations

When traveling to the Dominican Republic, it's essential to prioritize safety and take necessary health precautions to ensure a smooth and enjoyable trip. Here are some important considerations to keep in mind:

Health Precautions:
Vaccinations and Immunizations: Before embarking on your journey, consult with a healthcare professional or visit a travel clinic to receive recommended vaccinations. Common vaccinations include Hepatitis A and B, typhoid, and routine immunizations.

Water and Food Safety: While tap water in major cities is generally safe for drinking, it's advisable to consume bottled or filtered water, especially in more remote areas. When dining out, choose reputable establishments to reduce the risk of foodborne illnesses.

Mosquito-Borne Diseases: The Dominican Republic is in a region where mosquito-borne illnesses like dengue fever, chikungunya, and Zika virus are present. Pack and use insect repellent with DEET, wear long-sleeved shirts and long pants, and consider staying in accommodations with screens or air conditioning.

Sun Protection: The tropical climate means intense sun exposure. Bring and regularly apply sunscreen with a high SPF rating, wear a wide-brimmed hat, and seek shade during peak sun hours.

Medical Facilities: While there are hospitals and clinics in major cities, medical facilities in remote areas may be limited. It's wise to have travel insurance that covers medical emergencies and consider locating the nearest medical facility to your accommodation upon arrival.

Safety Tips:
Crime Awareness: Like any destination, it's important to be mindful of your surroundings and take precautions against petty crimes. Avoid displaying valuable items, use hotel safes, and be cautious in crowded or tourist-heavy areas.

Transportation Safety: If renting a vehicle, ensure it's from a reputable agency and thoroughly inspect it before driving. Exercise caution on the roads, as driving habits may differ from what you're accustomed to. Utilize licensed taxi services or ridesharing apps for safe transportation.

Water Activities: When engaging in water-based activities such as swimming, snorkeling, or diving, adhere to safety guidelines provided by tour operators. Wear appropriate gear, follow instructions, and be aware of local currents and tides.

Natural Hazards: The Dominican Republic is susceptible to natural disasters like hurricanes. Monitor weather forecasts and follow any evacuation or safety advisories issued by local authorities.

Local Laws and Customs: Familiarize yourself with the local laws and customs to show respect for the culture. For instance, it's customary to greet with a handshake and say "Buenos días" (good morning) or "Buenas tardes" (good afternoon) as a sign of respect.

Remember, your safety and well-being are paramount. By taking these precautions, you can fully enjoy the rich experiences the Dominican Republic has to offer.

Language and Communication Tips

When traveling to the Dominican Republic, having some knowledge of the local language can greatly enhance your experience and interactions with locals. Spanish is the official language, and while many Dominicans in tourist areas speak some English, making an effort to communicate in Spanish is appreciated and often leads to more enriching encounters.

Learn Basic Spanish Phrases:
While you may not become fluent overnight, learning a few basic phrases can go a long way. Simple greetings like "Hola" (Hello), "Gracias" (Thank you), and "Por favor" (Please) can open doors and show respect for the local culture. Additionally, being able to ask for directions, order food, and handle basic transactions will make your journey smoother.

Practice Pronunciation:

Spanish pronunciation can be tricky, but putting effort into correct pronunciation shows respect for the language and its speakers. Pay attention to the sounds of letters and practice them regularly. Many language learning apps and websites offer audio resources for pronunciation practice.

Utilize Language Learning Apps:
There are several mobile applications designed to help travelers learn and practice languages. Apps like Duolingo, Babbel, and Rosetta Stone offer interactive lessons and exercises that can be incredibly useful for picking up basic conversational Spanish before and during your trip.

Engage Locals in Conversation:
Don't be shy about striking up conversations with locals. Dominicans are generally warm and welcoming, and they appreciate when visitors make an effort to communicate in Spanish. Even if you stumble over words, most people will be patient and appreciative of your attempt.

Use Translation Apps:
In moments where you find yourself struggling to communicate, consider using translation apps. Google Translate, for example, allows you to type or speak a phrase in your native language and have it translated into Spanish. This can be especially handy in situations where precision is crucial, such as when discussing dietary restrictions or medical needs.

Listen and Observe:
Pay attention to how locals speak, the expressions they use, and their body language. This can provide valuable insight into the nuances of the language and help you adapt your own communication style.

Be Mindful of Regional Dialects:

Keep in mind that the Dominican Republic, like many countries, has regional dialects and accents. While standard Spanish is understood across the country, you may notice some variations in pronunciation and vocabulary, especially in more rural or isolated areas.

By taking the time to learn some basic Spanish and practicing good communication habits, you'll not only enhance your travel experience but also forge deeper connections with the people you meet along the way. Remember, every effort you make to communicate in the local language is a sign of respect and appreciation for the Dominican culture.

Transportation Tips

Navigating through the Dominican Republic is an essential aspect of ensuring a smooth and enjoyable trip. Here are some valuable transportation tips to keep in mind:

1. Renting a Car:
Renting a car can be a convenient way to explore the Dominican Republic, especially if you plan on visiting remote areas or off-the-beaten-path destinations. Major cities like Santo Domingo, Punta Cana, and Santiago have reputable car rental agencies. However, be prepared for varying road conditions, and consider renting a 4-wheel drive for more challenging terrains.

2. Public Transportation:
The Dominican Republic has an extensive public transportation system. Buses and guaguas (shared minivans) are common modes of transport between cities and towns. Metro and bus services are available in major cities like Santo Domingo and Santiago. While economical, it's essential to be aware of schedules and potential delays.

3. Taxis and Ride-Sharing:
Taxis are widely available in urban areas and can be hailed from the street or booked through a hotel. Negotiating the fare beforehand is advisable. Ride-sharing apps like Uber and Lyft are also operational in certain cities, providing a convenient and often more transparent option.

4. Motorcycle Taxis (Motoconchos):
In many Dominican cities, especially in busy urban centers, motorcycle taxis are a popular mode of transportation. They can be a quick and affordable way to navigate through traffic. However, ensure you negotiate the fare upfront and prioritize safety by wearing a helmet.

5. Air Travel:
For longer distances or if you're pressed for time, consider domestic flights. The Dominican Republic has several airports, with major hubs in Santo Domingo, Punta Cana, and Santiago. This option is especially useful if you're planning to visit multiple regions of the country.

6. Ferry Services:
If you're looking to explore the nearby islands, such as Saona or Catalina, there are ferry services available. These offer a scenic way to reach these beautiful destinations, but it's advisable to check schedules in advance.

7. Driving Tips:
If you choose to rent a car, there are a few important things to keep in mind. Firstly, drive on the right side of the road. Additionally, be cautious of local driving habits, such as aggressive overtaking. Road signage can sometimes be limited, so having a GPS or navigation app is highly recommended.

8. Parking Considerations:

Finding parking in busy urban areas can be a challenge. Look for secure parking lots or garages, especially if you're leaving the vehicle overnight. In smaller towns, parking is generally easier to find.

9. Language Barrier:
While English is understood in tourist areas, having a basic grasp of Spanish can be immensely helpful when asking for directions or seeking assistance from locals.

By keeping these transportation tips in mind, you'll be better prepared to explore the diverse landscapes and attractions of the Dominican Republic.

Recommended Reading and Resources

"Lonely Planet Dominican Republic" by Lonely Planet

This comprehensive guide offers detailed information on attractions, accommodations, and cultural insights, making it an essential companion for travelers exploring the Dominican Republic.

"The Rough Guide to the Dominican Republic" by Rough Guides

With practical advice, maps, and insider tips, this guidebook is perfect for travelers seeking both adventure and cultural experiences.

"Moon Dominican Republic" by Lebawit Lily Girma

This guide is written by a travel expert who has a deep understanding of the country, offering unique perspectives and personalized recommendations.

Historical and Cultural Insights

"The Brief Wondrous Life of Oscar Wao" by Junot Díaz

This Pulitzer Prize-winning novel provides a vivid portrayal of Dominican-American experiences, blending history, culture, and personal narratives.

"The Feast of the Goat" by Mario Vargas Llosa

A historical novel depicting the final days of the Dominican Republic's dictator Rafael Trujillo, offering a gripping account of a critical period in the country's history.

Natural History and Ecology

"A Field Guide to the Birds of the Dominican Republic and Haiti" by Steven Latta, Christopher Rimmer, and others

This field guide is an excellent resource for birdwatchers, providing detailed information about the avian species found in the Dominican Republic.

"The Butterflies of Hispaniola" by David M. Wright and Alain H. Smith

For nature enthusiasts, this guide offers insights into the diverse butterfly species that inhabit the island.

Online Resources

GoDominicanRepublic.com

The official tourism website of the Dominican Republic provides a wealth of information on destinations, activities, and travel tips.

Dominican Today

A reliable source for news, events, and cultural happenings in the Dominican Republic, offering insights for both tourists and expatriates.

Travel Forums and Communities

TripAdvisor - Dominican Republic Forum

A vibrant community of travelers sharing experiences, tips, and recommendations about their trips to the Dominican Republic.

Lonely Planet Thorn Tree - Caribbean Islands

A forum dedicated to discussions about the Caribbean, where travelers often exchange valuable insights on visiting the Dominican Republic.

These recommended resources offer a wide range of perspectives and information sources for travelers interested in exploring the Dominican Republic. Whether you're seeking practical travel advice, historical context, or ecological insights, these books, websites, and forums can be invaluable companions on your journey.

Chapter 14: Travel Itinerary

Family Friendly Itinerary

The Dominican Republic, with its stunning beaches, rich history, and vibrant culture, offers a wealth of family-friendly activities. This itinerary is designed to make the most of your time in this diverse and beautiful country, ensuring that every member of the family has an unforgettable experience.

Day 1: Santo Domingo - Historical Exploration

Morning:
Begin your trip with a visit to the Zona Colonial in Santo Domingo. Explore the cobbled streets, historic buildings, and impressive cathedrals. Don't miss the Alcázar de Colón, a magnificent mansion turned museum.

Enjoy a family-friendly brunch at a local cafe, savoring Dominican flavors.

Afternoon:
Head to the Museum of the Royal Houses to learn about the island's colonial past. Engage the kids with interactive exhibits and guided tours tailored for young learners.

Take a stroll along the Malecón, a picturesque waterfront promenade, and enjoy street performances and vendors.

Evening:
Have dinner at a family-friendly restaurant in the Zona Colonial, where you can try local dishes like mangu or mofongo.

Consider attending a traditional dance performance or cultural show in the area.

Day 2: Punta Cana - Beaches and Water Adventures

Morning:
Arrive in Punta Cana, known for its pristine beaches. Spend the morning at Bavaro Beach, building sandcastles and swimming in the crystal-clear waters.
Engage in beach activities like snorkeling and paddleboarding. Many resorts offer equipment rentals and guided tours.

Afternoon:
Enjoy a delightful seafood lunch at a beachfront restaurant, offering a wide range of options for even the pickiest eaters.

Visit a local adventure park for exciting experiences like ziplining and nature trails.

Evening:
Participate in a family-friendly catamaran cruise. Sail along the coast, snorkel in the coral reefs, and enjoy a sunset dinner on board.

Day 3: Higuey - Cultural Experience and Wildlife Encounter

Morning:
Head to Basilica de Higuey. This impressive cathedral is a significant pilgrimage site and offers a glimpse into the local religious culture.

Afternoon:
Visit the Bavaro Adventure Park for a mix of eco-tourism and adventure activities. Kids can enjoy a range of supervised activities like bungee trampolines and a petting zoo.

Evening:

Have dinner at a local restaurant specializing in traditional Dominican cuisine. Consider trying local delicacies like mangu and tostones.

Day 4: Puerto Plata - Outdoor Excursions

Morning:
Explore the 27 Charcos de Damajagua, a series of stunning waterfalls. Older kids and adventurous adults can enjoy cliff jumping and natural water slides.

Afternoon:
Visit the Amber Museum in Puerto Plata. Discover the fascinating world of amber and its importance in the Dominican Republic's history.

Evening:
Stroll along the Malecón de Puerto Plata, where you'll find street vendors, live music, and local art displays. Enjoy dinner at a beachside restaurant.

Day 5: Samaná - Nature and Marine Life

Morning:
Take a guided tour to Los Haitises National Park. Explore the mangrove forests, caves with Taino petroglyphs, and birdwatching opportunities.

Afternoon:
Head to the El Limón Waterfall, a stunning natural wonder.

Hike or ride horseback to reach the falls, then cool off in the refreshing pool.

Evening:

Join a whale-watching excursion (seasonal) in Samaná Bay. Witness the incredible humpback whales in their natural habitat.

Day 6: Punta Cana - Adventure and Relaxation
Morning:

For a thrilling adventure, embark on a family-friendly ATV or dune buggy tour through the rugged terrain of Punta Cana.
Afternoon:

Enjoy a leisurely afternoon at the resort. Take advantage of the pool, water sports, and organized activities for kids.

Evening:

Have a farewell dinner at one of Punta Cana's fine dining restaurants, celebrating the wonderful memories created during your trip.

This family-friendly itinerary ensures a perfect blend of cultural immersion, outdoor adventures, and relaxation in the Dominican Republic. From historic exploration in Santo Domingo to beach fun in Punta Cana, every day offers a new and exciting experience for the entire family to cherish. Enjoy your trip!

Art and Culture Itinerary

This itinerary is designed for travelers seeking to immerse themselves in the art and culture of the Dominican Republic. Each day is curated to provide a comprehensive experience, from exploring historical sites to engaging with local artisans.

Day 1: Santo Domingo - The Colonial City

Morning

Visit Alcázar de Colón: Begin your cultural journey at this historical landmark, once the residence of Christopher Columbus' son Diego. Explore the beautifully preserved rooms and courtyards that offer a glimpse into colonial life.

Catedral Primada de América: Adjacent to the Alcázar, this cathedral is the oldest in the Americas. Its stunning Gothic and Renaissance architecture is a testament to the city's rich religious history.

Afternoon

Museo de las Casas Reales: Discover the extensive collection of artifacts and exhibits that narrate the history of colonial Santo Domingo, showcasing the interactions between European, African, and Indigenous cultures.

Lunch at Plaza España: Enjoy a meal at one of the charming restaurants in this lively square, surrounded by historical buildings and vibrant street performers.

Evening

Paseo de la Atarazana: Take a leisurely stroll along this scenic waterfront promenade, lined with galleries and workshops, showcasing the talents of local artists.

Dinner at a Colonial Restaurant: Indulge in traditional Dominican cuisine in an atmospheric colonial setting.

Day 2: Altos de Chavón and La Romana
Morning

Altos de Chavón: Explore this picturesque Mediterranean-style village perched on a cliff above the Chavón River. Visit the Regional Museum and the School of Design, where local artisans create impressive works.

Amphitheater: If possible, catch a live performance at the amphitheater, which has hosted renowned artists from around the world.

Afternoon

Chavón River Cruise: Embark on a scenic boat ride along the Chavón River, offering breathtaking views of the surrounding countryside.

Lunch at La Romana: Enjoy fresh seafood and local delicacies in La Romana, a charming coastal town.

Evening

Cigar Factory Tour: Learn about the Dominican Republic's renowned cigar-making industry at a local factory. Witness skilled craftsmen at work and gain insights into the production process.

Dinner in La Romana: Savor a meal in one of the town's waterfront restaurants, accompanied by the sound of the waves.

Day 3: Puerto Plata and Santiago
Morning

Amber Museum (Museo del Ámbar): Begin your day in Puerto Plata by exploring the fascinating world of amber. This museum houses an extensive collection of amber specimens, some of which contain ancient plant and insect inclusions.

Teleférico de Puerto Plata: Take a cable car ride up to the peak of Mount Isabel de Torres, offering panoramic views of Puerto Plata and the surrounding coastline.

Afternoon

Fort of San Felipe: Delve into the history of Puerto Plata at this 16th-century fort. Explore its ramparts and learn about its role in defending the city.

Lunch at the Malecón: Enjoy a meal at one of the seafood restaurants along the Malecón, while taking in the views of the Atlantic Ocean.

Evening

Travel to Santiago: Head to Santiago, the cultural capital of the Dominican Republic, known for its vibrant arts scene.

Cultural Show or Concert: Depending on the schedule, attend a local cultural performance or concert, showcasing the diverse talents of Dominican artists.

Day 4: Santiago - City of the 30 Heroes
Morning

Centro León: Immerse yourself in the dynamic arts and culture scene of Santiago at this contemporary cultural center. Explore its galleries, exhibitions, and attend workshops or lectures.

Kandela Art Space: Visit this dynamic cultural hub where local artists create and showcase their works, providing a glimpse into the thriving arts community.

Afternoon
Lunch in Santiago: Savor traditional Dominican cuisine at one of the city's renowned eateries.

Mural Tour: Embark on a guided tour of Santiago's vibrant street art scene, exploring the murals that adorn the city's walls, each telling a unique story.

Evening

Dinner and Live Music: Enjoy a lively evening at a local restaurant featuring live music, showcasing the diverse musical traditions of the Dominican Republic.
Conclusion

This four-day itinerary offers a deep dive into the art and culture of the Dominican Republic, allowing travelers to engage with history, explore contemporary artistic expressions, and connect with the local creative community. From colonial cities to vibrant cultural hubs, this journey provides a comprehensive experience of the island's rich and diverse cultural heritage.

Romantic Itinerary

Day 1: Arrival in Paradise - Punta Cana

Morning:
Arrive at Punta Cana International Airport, where a private transfer takes you to your luxurious beachfront resort.

Enjoy a welcome brunch overlooking the pristine beaches and turquoise waters.

Afternoon:
Unwind together with a couples' massage at the resort's spa, complete with aromatherapy and a jacuzzi soak.
Stroll hand in hand along Bavaro Beach, renowned for its powdery white sand and swaying palm trees.

Evening:
Indulge in a candlelit dinner at a beachfront restaurant, savoring fresh seafood and local delicacies.

Dance the night away to live music or enjoy a private moonlit walk on the beach.

Day 2: Island Adventure - Saona Island
Morning:

Embark on a private catamaran tour to Saona Island, a secluded paradise known for its serene beaches and crystal-clear waters.

Snorkel together in the vibrant coral reefs, hand in hand, marveling at the colorful marine life.

Afternoon:
Enjoy a beachfront picnic, featuring gourmet cuisine and tropical fruits, with the sound of the waves as your backdrop.

Take a romantic stroll through the coconut groves and explore the island's natural beauty.

Evening:
Return to your resort in time for a private sunset dinner on the beach, with a bonfire and personalized service.

Day 3: Historical Romance - Santo Domingo
Morning:

Travel to Santo Domingo, the capital city, and check into a charming boutique hotel in the historic Zona Colonial.
Visit the Alcázar de Colón, a 16th-century palace, and immerse yourselves in the rich history of the island.

Afternoon:
Explore Calle El Conde, a bustling street lined with shops, cafes, and historic landmarks, perfect for a leisurely stroll and people-watching.

Discover the Cathedral of Santa María la Menor, the oldest cathedral in the Americas, and revel in its awe-inspiring architecture.

Evening:
Dine at a romantic rooftop restaurant, offering panoramic views of the city and a delectable fusion of Caribbean and Spanish flavors.

Day 4: Secluded Retreat - Jarabacoa
Morning:

Travel to Jarabacoa, a picturesque mountain town known for its lush landscapes and serene ambiance.

Check into a cozy mountain cabin or boutique eco-lodge, surrounded by breathtaking nature.

Afternoon:
Embark on a private horseback ride through the scenic countryside, exploring waterfalls and hidden trails.

Share a quiet picnic by the mesmerizing Jimenoa Waterfall, listening to the soothing sounds of nature.

Evening:
Enjoy a candlelit dinner at your retreat, with a menu featuring fresh, locally-sourced ingredients and mountain-inspired dishes.

Day 5: Adventure and Relaxation - Samaná Peninsula

Morning:
Head to the Samaná Peninsula, renowned for its stunning landscapes and vibrant culture.

Take a boat tour to El Limón Waterfall, a breathtaking cascade nestled in the heart of the jungle.

Afternoon:
Relish a seafood lunch on the beach in Las Terrenas, a charming coastal town known for its laid-back atmosphere.

Spend the afternoon lounging on the beach or indulging in a couple's spa treatment.

Evening:
Dine at a beachfront restaurant, where the soft glow of lanterns sets the mood for an intimate evening.

Day 6: Sunset Magic - Cabarete

Morning:
Drive to Cabarete, a coastal town known for its vibrant atmosphere and water sports.

Check into a beachfront resort with stunning views of the ocean.

Afternoon:

Try tandem kite surfing or windsurfing lessons for an exhilarating adventure on the water.

Explore the local art galleries and boutiques, where you can find unique souvenirs and keepsakes.

Evening:
Witness a mesmerizing sunset at Kite Beach, where the colors of the sky paint a romantic backdrop.

Dine at a beachside restaurant, indulging in fresh seafood and sipping cocktails under the starlit sky.

Day 7: Farewell, but not Goodbye

Morning:
Enjoy a leisurely breakfast on the terrace, savoring your last moments in paradise.

Take a scenic drive to the airport, reminiscing about the unforgettable experiences you've shared.

Afternoon:
Depart from Punta Cana International Airport, carrying with you memories of a truly magical romantic getaway.

Notes for Your Romantic Getaway:

Private Moments: Throughout the trip, take time for private moments - a quiet beach walk, a secluded dinner, or a shared adventure just for two.

Customized Experiences: Consider personalizing the itinerary with surprise activities or special arrangements to make the trip uniquely yours.

Cuisine and Dining: Explore local flavors and indulge in romantic dining experiences, from beachfront dinners to candlelit rooftop settings.

Capture Memories: Don't forget to capture the moments through photos or a travel journal, so you can relive the romance long after you return home.

Flexibility: While this itinerary provides a framework, feel free to adapt it based on your preferences and any unforeseen circumstances.

This romantic itinerary offers a perfect blend of adventure, relaxation, and cultural experiences, providing you and your partner with memories that will last a lifetime. Enjoy your romantic getaway in the Dominican Republic!

Food and Wine Itinerary
Day 1: Santo Domingo - Historic Flavors

Morning:
9:00 AM - Breakfast at La Briciola: Start your culinary journey with a hearty Dominican breakfast at La Briciola in the Zona Colonial. Indulge in Mangu (mashed plantains), eggs, and fried cheese, accompanied by a cup of rich Dominican coffee.

10:30 AM - Zona Colonial Walking Tour: Embark on a guided tour of the historic Zona Colonial. Along the way, sample local snacks like pastelón de plátano maduro (ripe plantain casserole) from street vendors.

Afternoon:
1:00 PM - Lunch at El Conuco: Head to El Conuco, a charming restaurant known for its traditional Dominican cuisine. Try the famous mofongo, a dish made of mashed plantains, and savor various local stews.
3:00 PM - Chocolate and Cigar Tour: Visit the KahKow Experience for a chocolate-making workshop. Learn about the cacao production process and enjoy a tasting session. Later, explore a cigar factory to witness the craftsmanship behind Dominican cigars.

Evening:
7:00 PM - Dinner at Mesón de Bari: Mesón de Bari offers a fusion of Spanish and Dominican flavors. Try the seafood paella paired with a crisp white wine. Don't forget to indulge in a refreshing passion fruit mojito.

Day 2: Punta Cana - Beachside Dining

Morning:
9:30 AM - Brunch at Jellyfish Restaurant: Enjoy brunch by the sea at Jellyfish Restaurant. Relish fresh seafood dishes like ceviche and grilled lobster, complemented by tropical fruit juices.

11:30 AM - Beach Relaxation: Spend the mid-morning lounging on the pristine beaches of Punta Cana. Enjoy the sun, surf, and soft sands.

Afternoon:
1:30 PM - Cooking Class at La Yola: Participate in a hands-on cooking class at La Yola Restaurant. Learn to prepare local delicacies like mangu and yam cassava. Savor your creations with a glass of chilled Dominican rum.

4:00 PM - Catamaran Sunset Cruise: Embark on a catamaran cruise along the coast, enjoying breathtaking views of the sunset. Sip on cocktails and nibble on light snacks as you sail.

Evening:
8:00 PM - Dinner at Passion by Martin Berasategui: Experience world-class dining at Passion. Chef Martin Berasategui offers a gourmet tasting menu with wine pairings, providing a true culinary masterpiece.

Day 3: Santiago - Gastronomic Adventures
Morning:
10:00 AM - Mercado Modelo Visit: Explore Mercado Modelo, a bustling market in Santiago. Sample local fruits, spices, and snacks, and interact with vendors for an authentic Dominican experience.

12:00 PM - Lunch at Pica Pollo el Progreso: Savor the best pica pollo (fried chicken) in Santiago at this local favorite. The crispy, flavorful chicken is a must-try.

Afternoon:
2:00 PM - Visit to a Coffee Plantation: Head to a nearby coffee plantation for a tour. Learn about the coffee-making process and enjoy a freshly brewed cup of Dominican coffee.

4:30 PM - Rum Tasting at Brugal Rum Factory: Take a guided tour of the Brugal Rum Factory. Discover the history and craftsmanship behind one of the Dominican Republic's most renowned rum brands. Enjoy a tasting session of various aged rums.

Evening:
7:30 PM - Dinner at Mangu Restaurante & Bar: Indulge in a diverse menu of Dominican and international dishes at

Mangu. Try their signature mangu variations and pair it with a fine selection of wines.

Day 4: Puerto Plata - Coastal Flavors

Morning:

9:00 AM - Breakfast at Casa Azul: Enjoy a leisurely breakfast at Casa Azul, known for its Caribbean-inspired cuisine. Try their tropical fruit smoothie bowls and avocado toast.

11:00 AM - Visit to Amber Museum: Explore the Amber Museum to learn about the unique geological history of the region. Don't miss the stunning amber exhibits.

Afternoon:

1:30 PM - Lunch at El Manguito: Dine at El Manguito for a taste of fresh seafood and Creole specialties. Try the seafood stew and enjoy views of the ocean.

3:30 PM - Cable Car Ride to Pico Isabel de Torres: Take a cable car ride to the peak of Pico Isabel de Torres for panoramic views of Puerto Plata. Enjoy a snack at the mountaintop café.

Evening:

7:00 PM - Dinner at La Casita de Papi: Experience authentic Dominican cuisine at La Casita de Papi. Indulge in dishes like mofongo with shrimp or churrasco steak, accompanied by local rum cocktails.

This detailed itinerary offers a diverse range of culinary experiences, from historic flavors in Santo Domingo to beachside dining in Punta Cana, and gastronomic adventures in Santiago and Puerto Plata. Each day is filled with activities that immerse you in the rich food and wine culture of the Dominican Republic. Enjoy your culinary exploration!

Historical Itinerary

Day 1: Santo Domingo - The Colonial Capital
Morning:

8:00 AM: Start your day with a visit to the Zona Colonial, a UNESCO World Heritage Site. Explore the cobbled streets, admiring the well-preserved Spanish colonial architecture.

10:00 AM: Head to the Alcázar de Colón, the former residence of Christopher Columbus' son, Diego. Marvel at its grandeur and historical significance.

Lunch:

12:30 PM: Enjoy a leisurely lunch at a charming cafe within the Zona Colonial. Try local delicacies like mangu or mofongo.
Afternoon:

2:00 PM: Visit the Museo de las Casas Reales, an insightful museum showcasing the colonial history of the Dominican Republic.

4:00 PM: Take a guided tour of the Catedral Primada de América, the oldest cathedral in the Americas.

Evening:

6:30 PM: Have dinner at a rooftop restaurant, overlooking the beautifully lit colonial district.

Day 2: Exploring Historic Fortifications
Morning:

9:00 AM: Head to Fortaleza Ozama, a historic fort that has witnessed centuries of battles. Explore its ramparts and enjoy panoramic views of Santo Domingo.

11:00 AM: Visit Fort San Gil, a smaller fortification that played a crucial role in protecting the city.

Lunch:

1:00 PM: Enjoy a seafood lunch at a restaurant along the Malecón, overlooking the Caribbean Sea.
Afternoon:

3:00 PM: Explore the Casa de Tostado, a meticulously restored 16th-century home, showcasing the lifestyle of the colonial elite.

5:00 PM: Walk along the Malecón and enjoy the sea breeze, taking in the views of the historic district.

Evening:

7:00 PM: Dine at a restaurant specializing in Dominican cuisine and perhaps catch a live merengue performance.

Day 3: Altos de Chavón and La Romana
Morning:

8:00 AM: Depart for Altos de Chavón, a recreated 16th-century Mediterranean village perched above the Chavón River. Explore its cobblestone streets, art galleries, and the archaeological museum.

10:30 AM: Visit the Regional Archaeological Museum to learn about the pre-Columbian history of the Dominican Republic.

Lunch:

1:00 PM: Enjoy lunch at one of the village's charming restaurants overlooking the Chavón River.
Afternoon:

2:30 PM: Head to La Romana and visit the Altos de Chavón Amphitheater, an architectural gem where numerous international artists have performed.

4:30 PM: Explore the Museo del Ron (Rum Museum) and learn about the history of rum production in the Dominican Republic.

Evening:

6:30 PM: Enjoy dinner at a restaurant in La Romana, known for its fresh seafood.
Day 4: Puerto Plata - Historical North Coast
Morning:

9:00 AM: Explore the Fort of San Felipe, a 16th-century Spanish fortification overlooking the Atlantic Ocean.

11:00 AM: Visit the Museum of Amber to learn about the significance of amber in the region.

Lunch:

1:00 PM: Enjoy a Dominican lunch at a local restaurant near the Malecón in Puerto Plata.
Afternoon:

3:00 PM: Take the Puerto Plata Cable Car to the summit of Mount Isabel de Torres for breathtaking views of the city and coastline.

5:00 PM: Visit the Victorian District, known for its beautifully preserved 19th-century architecture.

Evening:

7:00 PM: Dine at a restaurant in the Victorian District, savoring both local and international cuisine.
Day 5: Santiago - Colonial Heartland
Morning:

8:30 AM: Visit the Monumento a los Héroes de la Restauración, an iconic landmark in Santiago, offering panoramic views of the city.

10:00 AM: Explore the Centro León, a cultural center with exhibits on Dominican art, history, and anthropology.

Lunch:

12:30 PM: Enjoy a Dominican lunch in Santiago's historic district.
Afternoon:

2:30 PM: Visit the Catedral de Santiago Apóstol, an architectural gem dating back to the 19th century.

4:00 PM: Explore the Museo Folklórico Don Tomás Morel, offering insights into local folklore and traditions.

Evening:

6:30 PM: Dine at a traditional Dominican restaurant, perhaps with live music reflecting the region's cultural heritage.

Remember this is just a guide, you can adjust to your taste!

Outdoor Adventure Itinerary

Day 1: Hiking and Waterfalls in El Limón

Morning

8:00 AM - Breakfast at Local Eatery
Start your day with a hearty Dominican breakfast featuring mangu, eggs, and fresh tropical fruits.

9:30 AM - Depart for El Limón
Journey to the El Limón waterfall located in the lush Samaná Peninsula.
Midday

10:30 AM - El Limón Waterfall Hike
Embark on a scenic hike through dense rainforest, guided by local experts. Encounter exotic flora and fauna along the way.

12:30 PM - Picnic Lunch by the Waterfall
Enjoy a packed lunch amidst the breathtaking natural beauty of El Limón.
Afternoon

2:00 PM - Horseback Riding Adventure
Experience a thrilling horseback ride back to the trailhead, offering a unique perspective of the surroundings.

4:00 PM - Refreshing Swim at El Limón

Cool off with a swim in the refreshing pool at the base of the waterfall.

Evening

7:00 PM - Seafood Dinner in Las Terrenas
Relish a delicious seafood dinner at a beachfront restaurant in Las Terrenas.

Day 2: Zip-Lining and White Water Rafting in Jarabacoa

Morning

8:00 AM - Breakfast at Mountain Lodge
Enjoy a hearty breakfast with mountain views at a cozy lodge in Jarabacoa.

9:30 AM - Zip-Lining Adventure
Embark on a thrilling zip-lining tour through the lush forests and over the Jarabacoa River.

Midday

12:30 PM - River Tubing Experience
Delight in a leisurely tubing adventure down the scenic Yaque del Norte River.

Afternoon

2:30 PM - White Water Rafting Excursion
Conquer the exhilarating rapids of the Yaque del Norte River with experienced guides.

Evening

7:00 PM - BBQ Dinner and Bonfire

Unwind with a sumptuous barbecue dinner and a bonfire at the lodge.

Day 3: Pico Duarte Expedition

Morning

6:00 AM - Breakfast and Packed Lunch Preparation
Fuel up with a hearty breakfast before setting off on the Pico Duarte expedition. Pack a nutritious lunch for the journey.

Midday

9:00 AM - Start the Pico Duarte Trek
Begin the challenging yet rewarding trek to the summit of Pico Duarte, the highest peak in the Caribbean.

Afternoon

1:00 PM - Picnic Lunch at La Compartición
Take a break and enjoy a well-deserved picnic lunch with stunning views.

Evening

5:00 PM - Set Up Camp at Valle de Lilís
Arrive at the picturesque Valle de Lilís, where you'll set up camp for the night.

Day 4: Descend from Pico Duarte and Waterfall Rappelling

Morning

7:00 AM - Descend from Pico Duarte

Descend from the peak and marvel at the incredible vistas along the way.

Midday

12:00 PM - Return to Base Camp
Arrive back at base camp and enjoy a well-deserved lunch.

Afternoon

2:30 PM - Waterfall Rappelling
Experience the adrenaline rush of rappelling down the cascading waterfalls of Baiguate.

Evening

7:00 PM - Celebratory Dinner in Jarabacoa
Reflect on your adventurous journey with a celebratory dinner at a local restaurant.

Day 5: River Rafting and Caving in Los Haitises National Park

Morning

8:00 AM - Depart for Los Haitises
Travel to Los Haitises National Park, a haven of biodiversity.

Midday

10:00 AM - River Rafting Adventure
Embark on a scenic river rafting tour through the park, witnessing its diverse wildlife and mangrove ecosystems.

Afternoon

1:00 PM - Cave Exploration

Explore the fascinating caves of Los Haitises, adorned with ancient Taino petroglyphs.

Evening

7:00 PM - Seafood Dinner in Sabana de la Mar
Relish a delightful seafood dinner in the coastal town of Sabana de la Mar.

This comprehensive itinerary provides a thrilling outdoor adventure experience in the Dominican Republic, ensuring a mix of adrenaline-pumping activities and serene natural encounters. Remember to check the weather conditions and local regulations before embarking on each adventure, and most importantly, have fun exploring this beautiful Caribbean destination!

Conclusion

As we reach the conclusion of this exhilarating journey through the Dominican Republic, it's evident that this enchanting Caribbean nation offers an abundance of experiences for every traveler. From the sun-drenched beaches to the rich tapestry of history, and the pulsating beats of its music to the warm hospitality of its people, the Dominican Republic stands as a treasure trove of fun and cool activities.

In these pages, we've explored not only the popular destinations but also uncovered hidden gems that promise unforgettable memories. Whether you seek adrenaline-pumping adventures or tranquil moments of relaxation, this diverse land caters to all tastes and preferences.

The Dominican Republic's natural beauty, from the crystal-clear waters that lap its shores to the lush mountains that dominate its interior, provides a canvas for countless adventures. You can dive into vibrant coral reefs, conquer mountain trails, or simply bask in the serenity of its secluded coves.

Moreover, the cultural richness of the Dominican Republic is palpable in every corner. The echoes of history reverberate through cobblestone streets, ancient ruins, and lively festivals. Engage with the locals, savor the flavors of their cuisine, and dance to the rhythms of merengue and bachata - these are experiences that will stay with you long after you leave.

The Dominican Republic is not just a destination; it's an immersion into a world of wonders. It invites you to step out of your comfort zone, to taste new flavors, and to embrace a culture that is as diverse as it is welcoming.

In closing, as you plan your adventure in this extraordinary country, remember that each experience is a brushstroke on the canvas of your memories. So, go forth, explore, indulge, and savor every moment. Let the Dominican Republic weave its magic, leaving you with a tapestry of cherished moments and a longing to return.

Embark on this journey with an open heart, for the Dominican Republic has a way of capturing souls and leaving an indelible mark on every traveler fortunate enough to set foot on its shores. It is, without a doubt, a destination that promises not just fun and cool activities, but a lifetime of treasured memories. Embrace the adventure, and let the Dominican Republic reveal its secrets to you.

Printed in Great Britain
by Amazon